Christmas Gifts
from the
Kitchen

Ideals Publishing Corp.
Milwaukee, Wisconsin

Contents

ISBN 0-89542-635-8

Copyright © MCMLXXVII by Ideals Publishing Corporation
Printed and bound in the U.S.A.
All rights reserved
Published by Ideals Publishing Corporation
11315 Watertown Plank Road
Milwaukee, Wisconsin 53226
Published simultaneously in Canada

Nut Roll, page 4

2

CANDIES

NUT ROLL

1 7½-oz. jar marshmallow creme
1 t. vanilla
3½ c. confectioners' sugar
1 lb. caramels
9½ c. chopped nuts

Combine marshmallow creme and vanilla; add sugar gradually. Shape into rolls about 1 inch in diameter. Wrap in plastic wrap and freeze for at least 6 hours. Melt caramels over hot water; keep warm. Dip candy rolls in caramels, then roll in nuts until well coated. Store cooled candy in a covered container. Makes about 5 pounds.

CHOCOLATE FUDGE

4½ c. sugar
   Dash salt
1 14½-oz. can (1⅔ c.) evaporated milk (undiluted)
2 T. butter
1 12-oz. package semisweet chocolate chips
3 packages (¼ lb. each) sweet cooking chocolate
1 1-pint jar marshmallow creme
2 T. vanilla
2 c. nutmeats (optional)

In a large heavy saucepan stir together sugar, salt, evaporated milk and butter. Stirring constantly, bring to a boil. Boil 7 minutes, stirring occasionally. Pour boiling hot syrup over both kinds of chocolate and marshmallow creme. Stir vigorously until chocolate melts. Add vanilla. Stir in nutmeats. Turn into buttered pan (9 x 9 x 1¾). Let stand in cool place to set. Refrigerate if necessary to keep firm, or store in tightly covered metal box.

Mrs. Charles W. Bailey

'SWONDERFUL CANDY

2 1-lb. boxes confectioners' sugar
12 oz. cream cheese, softened
½ c. finely chopped candied cherries
½ c. finely chopped nuts
   Almond or vanilla extract

Sift sugar. Mash cream cheese. Combine all ingredients, using 1 small bottle of extract or as much as desired. Knead as bread. Pack mixture into a square tin and chill in freezer before cutting.

Alba M. Wahl

APRICOT ACORNS

1 8-oz. can almond paste, crumbled
½ c. wheat germ
1 c. honey
½ c. sesame seeds
2 c. instant nonfat dry milk
36 dried apricots (about 8 oz.)
36 whole cloves

In a bowl, mix almond paste, wheat germ, honey, sesame seeds and milk powder until the mixture is smooth and thoroughly combined. Shape into 36 balls. Place apricot half on one side of each ball. Fasten apricot in place with a whole clove. Pinch the other side of the ball into a point to resemble an acorn. Place acorns side by side in a single layer on waxed paper or foil and let dry at room temperature. Store in an airtight container in a cool dry place until ready to serve.

PEANUT BUTTER KISSES

⅓ c. corn syrup
⅓ c. peanut butter
½ c. nonfat dry milk
⅓ c. confectioners' sugar
   Chopped nuts (optional)

In a small mixing bowl, combine corn syrup with peanut butter. When well mixed, gradually add nonfat dry milk and sifted confectioners' sugar. Shape into a roll about ¾ inch in diameter; roll in chopped nuts if desired. Wrap in waxed paper and chill. Cut into 24 one-inch pieces.

Rev. Amos L. Seldomridge

SNOW-WHITE FUDGE

3 c. sugar
1½ c. milk
¾ t. salt
3 T. butter or margarine
2 t. vanilla
½ c. chopped dried California apricots
½ c. marshmallow creme
⅓ c. chopped walnuts

Butter sides of 3-quart saucepan. Mix sugar, milk and salt in saucepan. Stir and heat until sugar dissolves and mixture boils. Cook, without stirring, to soft ball stage (238°). Stir in butter and vanilla. Place in pan of cold water and cool to lukewarm without stirring. Add apricots and beat until mixture holds shape. Stir in marshmallow creme and walnuts; beat until glossy. Spread fudge in buttered 9-inch square pan. When fudge sets, cut into 32 bars.

ORANGE CARAMEL FUDGE

3 c. sugar
½ c. hot water
1 c. evaporated milk
¼ t. salt
4 T. butter or margarine
2 t. grated orange rind
1 c. chopped nuts

Put 1 cup sugar in heavy saucepan. Cook and stir over medium heat until sugar is melted and golden colored. Add water and stir until sugar is dissolved. Stir in remaining sugar, milk and salt. Cook over low heat, stirring occasionally, until mixture reaches 242° on a candy thermometer. Remove from heat. Add butter, orange rind and nuts. Beat until thick and creamy. Turn into greased aluminum foil pan. Cool; mark into squares. Makes 1½ pounds.

Orange Caramel Fudge, this page

APRICOT SNOWBALLS

See color photo, page 35

2 c. uncrushed cornflakes (or bran or wheat flakes)
⅓ c. diced pitted dates
⅔ c. diced dried California apricots
½ c. chopped pecans
¼ c. honey
3 T. butter or margarine
1 t. vanilla
Granulated sugar (optional)
Strips of dried California apricots, red glacé cherry halves

Using a rolling pin, crush cornflakes between 2 sheets of waxed paper. Stir crushed cornflakes, dates, apricots and pecans until well mixed in large bowl. Melt honey and butter in small pan; blend in vanilla. Pour over cornflake mixture; mix thoroughly. Chill 30 minutes. Use 1 tablespoon of mixture to form each ball. Roll balls in sugar, if desired. Garnish each with a strip of apricot or a cherry half. Serve immediately or cover and chill until needed.

MELT-IN-THE MOUTH CARAMELS

1 c. butter or margarine
1 lb. brown sugar
Dash of salt
1 c. light corn syrup
1 14-oz. can sweetened condensed milk
1 t. vanilla

Melt butter in a heavy 3-quart saucepan. Add brown sugar and salt. Stir until thoroughly combined. Stir in corn syrup; mix well. Gradually add milk, stirring constantly. Cook and stir over medium heat until candy reaches firm ball stage (245° on candy thermometer), about 12 to 15 minutes. Remove from heat. Stir in vanilla. Pour in buttered 9 x 9 x 2-inch pan. Cool and cut into squares. Makes about 2½ pounds.

Mrs. Curtiss Mueller

MARZIPAN

8 oz. almond paste
¼ c. corn syrup
¾ c. marshmallow creme
1 lb. confectioners' sugar

Combine ingredients; blend with hands. Form into fruit shapes. Paint with food coloring dissolved in water.

PUDDING CANDY

1 3-oz. package pudding mix, any flavor (not instant)
1 c. sugar
½ c. evaporated milk
1 T. butter or margarine
1 T. salted peanuts
¼ t. vanilla
1 c. nuts or raisins or coconut

Combine pudding and sugar in saucepan; add milk and butter. Cook and stir over medium heat until mixture boils. Lower heat and boil for 3 minutes, stirring constantly. Remove from heat; add vanilla and nuts. Beat until mixture becomes dull. Drop from spoon onto waxed paper. Makes 2 dozen. *Note:* Try chocolate pudding with nuts or raisins; vanilla or lemon with coconut or almonds, butterscotch with pecans.

PRALINES

1½ t. baking soda
4 c. sugar
2 c. light cream or half-and-half
3 T. butter
4 c. shelled pecans

Combine sugar and soda in large saucepan. Add cream; stir until sugar is dissolved. Bring to a boil over medium heat, stirring; reduce heat. Cook until candy reaches soft ball stage (234°). Remove from heat; add butter. Stir in pecans; beat until thick enough to drop from spoon. Drop onto waxed paper. If candy thickens, add a tablespoonful of hot water. Cool candy until firm.

*Photo opposite
Caramel Turtles, page 8*

COCONUT BALLS

¾ c. mashed potatoes
4 c. coconut
1 1-lb. package confectioners' sugar
1 t. almond extract
2 T. butter
2 T. corn syrup
3 T. water
1 package chocolate frosting mix

Combine first 4 ingredients. Roll into balls, using 1 heaping teaspoonful for each. Refrigerate for at least 1 hour. Combine remaining ingredients in top of double boiler. Heat, stirring, for 5 minutes. Keeping chocolate mixture over hot water, dip coconut balls until thoroughly coated. Remove from chocolate and place on waxed paper. Refrigerate until hardened. Makes 5 dozen.

SKILLET CANDIES

1 c. melted butter
1½ c. light brown sugar
2 c. cut-up dates
2 T. milk
2 eggs, beaten
½ t. salt
1 c. chopped nuts
1 t. vanilla
4 c. crisp rice cereal
Coconut

Melt butter; add sugar and dates. Cook over low heat. Add milk and slowly stir in beaten eggs. Bring to a boil and boil for 3 minutes. Remove from heat. When cool, add nuts, vanilla and cereal. Stir to mix well. Use a teaspoon to form candy into balls. Roll in coconut. Makes about 6 dozen.

PEANUT BRITTLE

2 c. sugar
1 c. white corn syrup
½ c. water
¼ t. salt
1 t. butter
2 c. raw Spanish peanuts
2 t. baking soda

Using a large kettle, boil first 4 ingredients together until mixture reaches thread stage (238°). Then add butter and peanuts. Stir, cook until golden brown. (300°). Remove from heat and add baking soda. Mixture will bubble up. Mix well and pour onto a well-greased enamel tabletop to cool. As it cools, pull as thin as possible. When cool, break into pieces and store in an airtight container.

Mabel White Epling

CARAMEL TURTLES

See color photo, page 7

1 c. pecan halves
36 light caramels
½ c. sweet chocolate, melted

Grease cookie sheet. Arrange pecans (flat side down) in clusters of 4. Place 1 caramel on each cluster of pecans. Heat in 325° oven until caramels soften (4-8 minutes). Remove from the oven; flatten caramel with buttered spatula. Cool slightly and remove from pan to waxed paper. Swirl melted chocolate on top.

Terry Gibson

FRANCES' PECAN BALLS

1 7½-oz. jar marshmallow creme
3½ c. confectioners' sugar
1 t. vanilla
¼ t. almond extract
1 lb. caramels
10 c. chopped pecans

Combine marshmallow creme, sugar and flavorings. Knead until ingredients are blended and mixture is soft. Form into balls about the size of pecans or smaller. Cover with plastic wrap and chill thoroughly. Melt caramels in top of double boiler. Dip balls into melted caramels and then roll them in chopped nuts. Store covered with plastic wrap. Can be kept several weeks. Yield: 5 pounds or about 116 balls.

Mrs. Dwight K. Beam

OATMEAL SQUARES

1 c. flaked coconut
½ c. cocoa
3 c. rolled oats
½ c. chopped pecans
½ t. salt
2 c. sugar
½ c. milk
½ c. butter
1 t. vanilla

Combine coconut, oatmeal, pecans and salt in large mixing bowl. Place sugar, milk, butter and vanilla in a saucepan; heat to boiling point. Boil for 2 minutes. Pour over oatmeal mixture; blend well. Spread in foil-lined 11 x 7 x 1½-inch pan. Refrigerate. Cut into small squares. Makes about 5 dozen.

BOURBON BALLS

1 c. vanilla wafer crumbs
1 c. finely chopped pecans
1 c. confectioners' sugar
2 T. cocoa
¼ c. bourbon
1½ T. light corn syrup
Confectioners' sugar for rolling

Mix crumbs, pecans, sugar and cocoa. Blend bourbon and syrup. Combine mixtures. Shape into balls; roll in sugar. Refrigerate.

ENGLISH TOFFEE

1 c. sugar
1 c. butter
3 T. water
1 t. vanilla
1 c. semisweet chocolate bits
1 c. chopped nuts

Combine first 4 ingredients in a medium saucepan. Cook over low to medium heat, stirring constantly, to hard crack stage (300°-310°). Remove from heat and pour onto a greased cookie sheet. While hot cover with chocolate chips. Spread. Sprinkle with chopped nuts.

TAN FUDGE

2 c. sugar
1 c. milk
1 7-oz. jar marshmallow creme
1 12-oz. jar crunchy peanut butter
1 t. vanilla

Combine sugar and milk in a large, heavy saucepan. Slowly bring to a boil. Cook, stirring, to soft ball stage (238°). Remove from heat and add remaining ingredients. Beat until blended. Pour into a buttered 9-inch pan; cool. When fudge has set, cut into squares.

Mary Ida Hoffman

CANDY STICKS

2 c. sugar
½ c. water
½ c. light corn syrup
2 T. lemon juice
1½ T. lemon rind
1 t. flavoring
Food coloring

Combine sugar, water, corn syrup, lemon juice and lemon rind in a medium saucepan. Bring to a boil and continue boiling, without stirring, until mixture reaches crack stage (290°). Remove from heat and add flavoring and food coloring. Pour onto a buttered platter. When candy is cool enough to handle, pull and twist into canes or sticks. *Note:* Try peppermint extract with red food coloring, lemon with yellow and cinnamon with red or brown. (To color candy brown, combine red and yellow food coloring with a drop of blue.)

Lollipops

Follow directions for Candy Sticks. Immediately after removing candy from heat, pour into buttered molds. Insert stick; let harden.

9

LEMON FRUIT-JELL CANDY

See color photo, page 55

1 6-oz. bottle liquid fruit pectin
2 T. water
½ t. baking soda
1 c. sugar
1 c. light corn syrup
2 t. lemon extract
10 drops yellow food coloring
   Granulated sugar

Combine fruit pectin and water in 2-quart saucepan. Stir in baking soda. (Mixture will foam slightly.) Mix sugar and corn syrup in a large saucepan. Place both saucepans over high heat and cook both mixtures, stirring alternately, until foam has thinned from fruit pectin mixture and sugar mixture is boiling rapidly, 3 to 5 minutes. Pour fruit pectin mixture in a slow steady stream into boiling sugar mixture, stirring constantly. Boil and stir 1 minute longer. Remove from heat. Stir in lemon extract and yellow food coloring. Pour immediately into a buttered 9-inch square pan. Let stand at room temperature until mixture is cool and firm— about 3 hours. Invert pan onto waxed paper which has been sprinkled with granulated sugar. Cut candy into ¾-inch squares or shapes and roll in sugar. Allow candy to stand awhile; roll again in sugar to prevent stickiness. Let stand overnight, uncovered, at room temperature before packing or storing. Makes about 1 pound. *Note:* Candies may also be rolled in confectioners' sugar, colored sprinkles or crystal sugar, or dipped in melted semisweet chocolate.

MOLASSES TAFFY

½ c. butter or margarine
1 c. molasses
2 c. granulated sugar
¼ c. light corn syrup
1½ c. water

Combine all ingredients in large saucepan; cook and stir over medium heat until sugar dissolves. Continue cooking until mixture thickens; then lower heat and cook to hard ball stage (260°). Pour onto a greased baking sheet and cool slightly. Butter hands and pull candy until hard and light. Stretch into a rope; cut into pieces. Makes 1½ pounds.

CHERRY NUT FUDGE

See color photo opposite

2 c. granulated sugar
1 c. heavy cream
   Dash salt
⅛ t. salt
½ t. vanilla
½ c. chopped nuts
½ c. chopped maraschino cherries

Bring sugar, cream and dash of salt to a boil over moderate heat, stirring constantly. When boiling point is reached, add ⅛ teaspoon salt. Cook until mixture reaches soft-ball stage. Remove from heat and let stand until almost cold. Beat until mixture is thick and creamy. Cover with a damp cloth and let stand for ½ hour. Add vanilla, nuts and cherries and work in with hands. Press into a shallow, waxed-paper-lined pan. Makes about 1 pound.

CRANBERRY JELLY CANDY

See color photo, page 55

1 16-oz. can jellied cranberry sauce
3 3-oz. packages cherry, raspberry or
   orange flavor gelatin
1 c. sugar
½ bottle liquid fruit pectin (3 fl. oz.)
1 c. chopped nuts or cookie coconut
   (optional)
   Additional sugar or flaked or cookie
   coconut

Beat cranberry sauce in a saucepan until smooth. Bring to a boil. Stir in gelatin and sugar; simmer 10 minutes, stirring frequently until gelatin is dissolved. Remove from heat. Stir in fruit pectin; then add nuts and stir 10 minutes to prevent nuts from floating. Pour into buttered 9-inch square pan. Chill until firm, about 2 hours. Invert onto waxed paper, which has been sprinkled with additional sugar. Cut candy into ¾-inch squares with spatula dipped in warm water; roll in sugar. After about an hour, roll in sugar again to prevent stickiness. Makes about 2 pounds candy.

SEAFOAM

2½ c. white sugar
½ c. dark corn syrup
½ c. water
2 egg whites
½ c. chopped nuts

Boil sugar, syrup and water until mixture reaches hard crack stage. Beat the egg whites until very stiff. Pour hot syrup slowly over egg whites with the mixer running at high speed. Then beat until stiff enough to drop. Add nuts and drop onto wax paper. Work quickly as mixture thickens rapidly.

Betty Bonkoski

HOLIDAY MINTS

3 egg whites
6 c. confectioners' sugar
Red and green food coloring
½ t. peppermint extract
½ t. spearmint extract

Beat egg whites until stiff, adding sugar gradually. Divide candy into 2 portions. Tint half green and half red. Add peppermint extract to red mixture and spearmint extract to green mixture. Roll candy between 2 pieces of waxed paper. Cut with small round cookie cutter. Let dry overnight.

CHOCOLATE-COVERED CHERRIES

1 8-oz. jar maraschino cherries with stems
½ recipe Chocolate Fudge (p. 3)

Drain cherries thoroughly. Prepare fudge according to directions, adding enough water to make dipping consistency. Put fudge in double boiler over hot water. Dip each cherry, leaving stem exposed. Place dipped cherries on waxed paper and cool until fudge sets. Store in a covered container in a cool place.

CANDIED ORANGE PEEL

7 large oranges
1½ c. water
2 c. sugar
3 T. honey
¼ t. salt
1 t. unflavored gelatin
Sugar

Cut oranges into fourths. Remove pulp and scrape away white membrane. Cut peel into strips. Place peel in saucepan, cover with water and simmer 15 minutes. Drain. Pour 1½ cups water over peel. Add 2 cups sugar, honey and salt. Cook over low heat for 45 minutes, stirring occasionally. Soften gelatin in ¼ cup water. Remove orange mixture from heat; add softened gelatin. Stir to dissolve. When cool, drain candy; roll in sugar. Let dry overnight on waxed paper. Store in a covered container. Makes about ¾ pound.

CARAMEL CORN

4 c. popped corn
½ c. almonds
½ c. pecans
½ c. butter or margarine
¼ c. light corn syrup
⅔ c. sugar

Combine popped corn and nuts; spread on an ungreased baking sheet. Melt margarine; stir in corn syrup and sugar. Bring to a boil over medium heat, stirring constantly. Continue boiling for 10 to 15 minutes, stirring occasionally. When mixture turns a light caramel color, remove from heat and stir in vanilla. Pour over corn and nuts and mix until all pieces are coated. Spread out to dry. Break into pieces and store in a covered container. Makes 1 pound.

GLAZED NUTS

2 T. cold water
1 egg white, slightly beaten
½ c. sugar
½ t. salt
¼ t. cinnamon
¼ t. cloves
¼ t. allspice
2 c. whole pecans

Add water to egg white. Stir in sugar, salt and spices. Mix well. Add nuts and stir until coated. Place nuts, flat side down, on a greased cookie sheet. Bake at 250° for 1 hour. Remove from pan immediately.

TOASTED ALMOND BALLS

1 c. semisweet chocolate bits
1 c. butterscotch bits
¾ c. confectioners' sugar
½ c. cultured sour cream
1½ t. grated orange rind
¼ t. salt
2 c. vanilla wafer crumbs
¾ c. finely chopped toasted almonds

Melt chocolate and butterscotch bits at a low heat. Mix in sugar, sour cream, orange rind, salt and crumbs; chill. Shape into ¾-inch balls; roll in almonds. Makes about 6½ dozen.

QUICK FONDANT WAFERS

1 6-oz. bottle liquid fruit pectin
3 lbs. confectioners' sugar
½ t. peppermint, rum, almond or orange extract (optional)
6 drops food coloring (optional)

Pour fruit pectin into a bowl. Gradually add 2 pounds confectioners' sugar, mixing well after each addition. (Mixture will be very stiff.) Divide into four parts; wrap in waxed paper or cover with a wet cloth. The remaining 1 pound confectioners' sugar will be used to dust board and rolling pin. Place ¼ of the fondant at a time on a pastry board, well dusted with sugar. Add flavoring and food coloring, if desired. Knead until smooth, adding sugar to board as needed and lifting with a spatula to prevent sticking. (Any unrolled portion may be wrapped in waxed paper or plastic wrap and stored at room temperature overnight.) Roll out with sugar-dusted rolling pin, about ¼ inch thick, turning often and dusting with sugar to prevent sticking. Cut out with cookie cutters dipped in confectioners' sugar. If desired, make a small hole at top of each wafer with a wooden pick. Place, top side down, onto waxed paper on baking sheets or trays. Press trimmings together; knead again until smooth, roll and cut, or shape into small balls. Allow to dry, uncovered, for 24 hours, turning once. Pack wafers in layers between waxed paper in a loosely covered box. Makes about 2¾ pounds. *Note:* To tint and flavor all the fondant the same, add 2 teaspoons extract and about 24 drops food coloring after cooling.

COCONUT CHRISTMAS COOKIE TREE

1½ c. butter or margarine
1 c. sugar
2 eggs
4½ c. sifted all-purpose flour
1 t. vanilla
1 t. almond extract
4 T. hot milk
1 lb. unsifted confectioners' sugar
Flaked coconut

Cut star-shaped patterns from heavy paper 9, 8, 7¼, 6½, 5½, 4¾, 4, and 3 inches in diameter, measuring from point to point. Cut two round patterns 2½ and 1½ inches in diameter.

Cream butter until soft. Gradually add sugar, beating until light and fluffy. Add eggs and beat well. Add flour, a small amount at a time, mixing thoroughly after each addition. Blend in vanilla, almond extract and 2 cups of the coconut (cut). Divide dough into 2 equal portions, wrap in waxed paper and chill at least 30 minutes or until firm enough to roll.

Roll dough ⅛-inch thick on a lightly floured board. Cut 2 cookies from each star pattern, making a total of 16 cookies. Cut 12 cookies from the 1½-inch round pattern and 20 cookies from the 2½-inch round pattern. With a large drinking straw, cut a hole in the center of each cookie. Place on ungreased baking sheets. Bake at 350° for about 8 minutes, or until edges are lightly browned. Cool.

Gradually add hot milk to the confectioners' sugar, using just enough milk for a spreading consistency. Tint green with food coloring if desired. Spread on each star-shaped cookie. Sprinkle flaked coconut near edges.

TO MAKE TREE

Place a 12- to 15-inch stick or thin candle in a candle holder. Secure with short stub of a candle or with paper. Slip 2 of the larger round cookies over stick. Top with largest star cookie and decrease to smallest size, placing 2 round cookies between each star-shaped cookie. Top with a rosette of frosting or a small candle. Decorate with silver dragées or small candles if desired. Makes 1 cookie tree.

COOKIES

STRIPED COOKIES

2½ c. sifted cake flour
1 t. double-acting baking powder
½ t. salt
½ c. butter or margarine
⅔ c. sugar
1 egg
1 T. milk
1 square unsweetened chocolate, melted
Milk

Sift flour with baking powder and salt. Cream butter. Gradually add sugar. Beat until light and fluffy. Add egg and milk. Blend well. Add flour mixture, a small amount at a time, beating well after each addition. Divide dough in half. Blend chocolate into one half. If necessary chill or freeze both parts of dough until firm enough to roll.

Roll each portion of dough on a lightly floured board into a 9 x 4½-inch rectangle. Brush chocolate dough lightly with milk and top with plain dough. Using a long, sharp knife, cut rectangle lengthwise in 3 equal strips 1½ inches wide.

Stack strips, alternating colors, brushing each layer with milk and pressing together lightly. Carefully wrap in waxed paper. Freeze until firm enough to slice, or chill overnight in refrigerator.

Cut in ⅛-inch slices, using a very sharp knife. Place on greased baking sheets. Bake at 400° for 6 to 8 minutes or just until white portions begin to brown. Makes about 5½ dozen.

SISTER JOAN'S CHRISTMAS COOKIES

2 c. broken nutmeats (walnuts or pecans)
1 lb. pitted dates cut into large pieces
½ c. dark seedless raisins
1 10-12 oz. jar maraschino cherries, cut in half
1 lb. dark brown sugar (not granulated)
½ c. butter or margarine
½ c. shortening
4 eggs
1¼ t. nutmeg
1 t. allspice
1 t. cinnamon
1 t. salt
1 t. baking soda
2 t. warm water
3 to 4 c. flour

Dissolve baking soda in warm water. Melt butter and shortening in large pan. Cool slightly and add brown sugar. Stir until dissolved. Stir in the following, beating well after each addition: baking soda and water; salt and spices; eggs (mix them in very well); fruit and nuts which have been cut up and dusted lightly with flour. Add flour until dough is just stiff enough to hold shape on spoon (drop cookie consistency). Drop from teaspoon onto greased and floured baking sheet. Bake in 350° oven for about 12-15 minutes until cookies spring back when pressed lightly. Cool. Makes 100 cookies.

Mrs. C. M. Stearns

LEMON FROSTED PECAN COOKIES

1 c. butter or margarine	1½ c. sifted flour
¾ c. sifted powdered sugar	¾ c. sifted cornstarch
2 T. milk	¾ c. chopped pecans

Mix and drop on cookie sheets. Bake at 400° for about 10 minutes. Cool and frost with 2 cups sifted powdered sugar, 4 tablespoons soft butter, 3 tablespoons lemon juice. Add a few drops of yellow food coloring if desired. Makes 5 to 6 dozen cookies.

Mrs. Robert Durkee

PEPPERMINT DELIGHTS

1 c. butter or margarine
1 c. sifted confectioners' sugar
2 t. vanilla
1½ c. sifted flour
½ t. salt
1 c. quick-cooking rolled oats
¼ c. crushed peppermint candy

Cream butter, add sugar and cream until fluffy. Add vanilla. Sift flour and salt together; add to creamed mixture. Fold in rolled oats and candy, mixing until dough holds together. Tint with red or green food coloring if desired. Roll out ⅛ inch thick on a board sprinkled with confectioners' sugar. Cut out cookies, sprinkle lightly with sugar and place on ungreased cookie sheets. Bake at 325° for 15 minutes. Makes 3 dozen cookies.

Clarence Ciolek

STIR-AND-DROP COOKIES

2 eggs
⅔ c. cooking oil
2 t. vanilla
1 t. grated lemon rind *or* 1 t. almond flavoring
¾ c. granulated sugar
2 c. flour
2 t. baking powder
½ t. salt

Heat oven to 400°. Beat eggs until blended. Stir in oil and flavorings. Blend in sugar until mixture thickens. Sift dry ingredients and add to mixture. Drop by teaspoonfuls about 2 inches apart on ungreased cookie sheet. Stamp each cookie with bottom of glass dipped in sugar. Decorate as you wish. Bake until cookies get a very light brown around the edges. Makes 3 to 5 dozen cookies. *Decorating ideas:* Place pecan half on cookie before baking. Or after cookies cool, frost with confectioners' sugar icing and top with assorted colored sprinkles.

Mr. & Mrs. Richard Davis

JEWELED SPICE BARS

    1 8-oz. package cream cheese
    ½ c. margarine
    1½ c. brown sugar, packed
    1 egg
    ¼ c. honey
    2¼ c. sifted flour
    1½ t. baking powder
    1 t. salt
    1 t. cinnamon
    1 t. nutmeg
    1 c. chopped nuts
    1 c. chopped candied fruit
    ½ c. raisins

Combine softened cream cheese, margarine, sugar and egg. Mix well. Stir in honey.
Sift together flour, baking powder, salt,
cinnamon and nutmeg. Add nuts, candied
fruit and raisins. Toss lightly to coat fruit.
Gradually add to cream cheese mixture.
Pour into greased and floured pan, 15 x 10½
inches. Bake at 350° for 30 to 35 minutes.

CONFECTIONERS' SUGAR ICING

    1⅓ c. sifted confectioners' sugar
    2 T. milk
    ¼ t. vanilla

Drizzle over warm bars. Cool. Cut into 3 x
1-inch bars. Makes 50.

Beth Green

WALNUT STRIPS

    1 c. butter or margarine
    1 c. sugar
    1 egg, separated
    2 c. flour
    ½ t. cinnamon
    1 T. water
    ½ c. finely chopped walnuts

Mix butter, sugar and egg yolk; beat well.
Combine flour and cinnamon; add to butter
mixture. Pat dough into a pan, 15½ x 10½
inches. Beat egg white and water until
foamy. Spread over dough. Sprinkle walnuts on top. Bake for 20 to 25 minutes at
350°. Cut into thin strips.

PACKING COOKIES FOR MAILING

Soft bar and drop cookies
usually travel well. Rolled or
pressed cookies break more
easily—they may become
crumbs before the recipient
gets them. Pack cookies of the
same variety together. Otherwise the flavors will mingle
and the distinctive taste of each
kind will be lost.

For best results, wrap cookies
singly or in pairs with plastic
wrap. Pack them in layers,
cushioning each row of cookies
with a generous layer of filler
such as popped corn or
crumpled newspaper. Use a
heavy cardboard box that will
not be crushed before it
reaches its destination. Add
enough filler so the box is very
full—the cookies should not
have room to bounce around
inside.

Label the package clearly. As a
safety precaution, enclose an
extra address label inside the
package. Be sure to use
adequate postage and to label
the package "FRAGILE." If you
wish, decorate the outside of
the box with bright holiday
stickers.

GINGERBREAD COOKIE BOX

See color photo opposite

GINGERBREAD CUTOUTS

1 c. butter
1 c. sugar
1 egg
1 c. dark molasses
2 T. vinegar
5 c. sifted flour
1½ t. baking soda
½ t. salt
2 t. ginger
1 t. cinnamon
1 t. cloves

Cream butter; add sugar gradually. Beat in egg, molasses and vinegar. Blend in sifted dry ingredients. Chill. Roll ⅛ to ¼ inch thick on floured surface; cut into desired shapes. Place on greased cookie sheets. Bake at 375° for 5 to 15 minutes depending on size and thickness of cookie.

SYRUP

1½ c. sugar
½ c. water
¼ c. light corn syrup

Combine all ingredients in a saucepan. Cover; bring to a boil; boil 5 minutes. Remove cover. Cook to 300° or hard crack stage. Switch to a warm heat setting to keep syrup boiling hot while putting parts of Gingerbread Box together. Work as quickly as possible. If mixture gets too thick, add a small amount of light corn syrup, bring to boiling point.

DECORATING FROSTING

2 egg whites
2½ c. confectioners' sugar
¼ c. light corn syrup
Food coloring

Beat egg whites until they hold a soft peak. Add sugar gradually and beat until sugar is dissolved and frosting stands in peaks. Add syrup and beat one minute. Divide frosting into small portions. Color each amount as desired with food coloring. Add a few drops of water if a thinner frosting is needed. Keep well covered when not in use.

INSTRUCTIONS FOR MAKING GINGERBREAD BOX

Make cardboard patterns using the following dimensions.

Sides—8 x 2¼ inches
Ends—6 x 2¼ inches
Bottom—8 x 5¾ inches
Top—8½ x 6¼ inches

Use Gingerbread Cutouts recipe. Place patterns on dough; cut around patterns with a sharp knife. Cut 2 sides, 2 ends, 1 bottom and 1 top. Place on greased cookie sheets. Bake as directed in recipe. Trim edges that are not straight while cookies are hot; work carefully. Cool on cookie sheets. Join the sides and ends to bottom of box by applying syrup to the edges; hold in place a few minutes until syrup sets. Decorate edges of box with Decorating Frosting. Decorate cover of box as desired. Fill box with miniature cookies or small Gingerbread Cutout cookies. Place cover on box.

Make a show-off gift box for Christmas cookies from a greeting card box with a see-through lid. Cover the bottom of the box with Christmas wrapping paper.

Store soft cookies in tins, with a slice of apple added to keep them moist. Crisp cookies should be kept in boxes—or freeze them so they'll stay oven-fresh.

Give Sandbakels with a set of molds, Springerle with a Springerle rolling pin, or Spritz Butter Cookies with a cookie press. The lucky recipient will be able to recreate your gift time and time again.

For a special friend, give a cookie jar filled with home-made cookies. Or make your own jar: spray paint an empty coffee can and stencil on a holiday design or wish. For a lasting gift, use colors and designs that will harmonize with the recipient's kitchen.

When cookie recipes specify a varying amount of flour, add the minimum amount first. Then bake a test cookie. If the cookie spreads more than it should, add a few tablespoons of flour. If you've added too much flour, the cookie may crack. Soften the dough with a little cream.

Any rolled cookie can be made into a Christmas tree ornament. Cut a piece of string or thread for each cookie. Before baking the cookies, press each down onto both ends of a string.

APRICOT CALICO COOKIES

See color photo, page 42

- 2 16- to 17-oz. cans apricot halves, drained and pureed
- ½ c. apricot preserves
- ¼ c. cornstarch
- 2 T. lemon juice
- 2 18-oz. packages refrigerated oatmeal-raisin cookie dough *or* 2 16-oz. packages refrigerated chocolate chip cookie dough
- 1 3½-oz. container red candied cherries, halved
- 1 3½-oz. container green candied cherries, quartered

In medium saucepan, combine pureed apricots, preserves, cornstarch and lemon juice. Cook over medium heat, stirring constantly, until mixture thickens and begins to boil. Cover and chill. Meanwhile, pat cookie dough evenly on bottom and sides of an ungreased 15½ x 10½ x 1-inch baking sheet. Evenly spread with apricot mixture. Decorate tops of cookies with flowers, using 1 red cherry half for flower and 2 green cherry quarters for leaves. Arrange flowers in rows on apricot mixture, 9 on the 15-inch sides and 8 on the 10-inch sides. Bake at 350° for 40 minutes or until toothpick inserted in center comes out clean. Cool on wire rack. When cool, cut into 2 x 1-inch bars, one flower on each cookie. Makes 72 cookies.

BUTTERSCOTCH CRISPS

- 2 c. sifted flour
- ½ t. salt
- ¾ c. butter
- 1 c. brown sugar
- 1 egg
- 1 t. vanilla
- ½ c. chopped nuts

Cream butter. Gradually add brown sugar and cream well. Add egg, vanilla and nuts; blend thoroughly. Sift flour and salt together. Add to beaten mixture and blend well. Shape dough into balls, using about 1 teaspoonful of dough. (If necessary, chill dough first.) Place on ungreased cookie sheet. Flatten with glass dipped in sugar. Bake at 400° for 8-10 minutes. Makes about 4 dozen.

PECAN PIE BARS

1 c. sifted flour
½ c. rolled oats
¼ c. brown sugar, packed
½ c. butter
3 eggs
¾ c. light corn syrup
1 c. coarsely chopped pecans
1 t. vanilla
¼ t. salt
½ c. brown sugar, packed
1 T. flour

Combine 1 cup flour, oats and ¼ cup brown sugar; cut in butter with pastry blender until mixture resembles coarse crumbs. Press mixture into greased 9 x 9 x 2-inch pan. Bake at 350° about 15 minutes. Beat eggs slightly; add remaining ingredients; blend well. Pour over partially baked crust. Bake at 350° about 25 minutes. Cool to room temperature. Cut into bars. Makes about 3 dozen.

CHOCOLATE PIXIES

2 c. sifted flour
¾ t. salt
2 t. baking powder
½ c. salad oil
4 oz. unsweetened chocolate, melted and cooled
2 c. granulated sugar
4 eggs
2 t. vanilla
½ c. chopped nuts
1 c. confectioners' sugar

Combine and sift flour, salt and baking powder. Mix in oil, melted chocolate and granulated sugar. Add eggs one at a time and mix well after each. Add vanilla and nuts and mix just until ingredients are combined. Chill for 1 hour. Using a tablespoon, drop batter into confectioners' sugar and shape into a ball. Place cookies about 2 inches apart on lightly greased cookie sheet. Bake at 350° for about 12 minutes. Makes about 4 dozen cookies.

Terry Jo Gibson

HONEY COOKIES

1 qt. honey
2 c. sugar
4 c. flour
1 c. butter
1 c. water
1 t. cinnamon
½ t. pepper
1 t. crushed cardamom seed
2 eggs, beaten
½ lb. nutmeats, finely chopped
1¼ T. baking soda
1 t. vanilla
8 c. flour

Cook honey and sugar together for 1 minute. Pour mixture over flour. Beat well, then add butter and water. Cool overnight. Then add next 7 ingredients and mix well. Add half of remaining flour. Chill. Add last 4 cups of flour when ready to roll cookies out. Roll and bake at 400° just until cookies begin to brown.

Mrs. Carlton Mueller

DREAM BARS

½ c. butter
1½ c. brown sugar
1⅛ c. flour
2 eggs
1 t. vanilla
½ t. baking powder
¼ t. salt
1½ c. shredded coconut
1 c. nutmeats

Cream butter, add ½ cup of brown sugar and beat well. Blend in 1 cup of flour and spread mixture in a large pan, about 9 x 13 inches. Bake for 15 minutes at 325°. Beat eggs with remaining brown sugar; add vanilla. Add remaining flour, baking powder, salt, coconut and nuts. Spread over baked layer. Return to oven and bake 25 additional minutes. Cut into bars while warm.

SPRINGERLE

4 eggs
2 c. sugar
4½ c. flour
Anise seed

Beat eggs until light and creamy. Add sugar gradually, beating until dissolved. Stir in flour until well blended. Chill several hours or overnight. Roll out ⅛ inch thick. If desired, press a floured springerle rolling pin on dough to emboss designs. Cut into squares. Transfer cookies onto a board that has been sprinkled with anise seed and additional flour. Let dry for 12 hours. Place cookies on greased baking sheet. Bake at 325° for 12 to 15 minutes. Makes about 9 dozen cookies.

LIZZIES

1½ c. sifted flour
1½ t. baking soda
1 t. cinnamon
¼ t. nutmeg
¼ t. cloves
¼ c. butter
½ c. brown sugar, packed
2 eggs
1½ T. milk
⅓ c. bourbon
1 lb. seeded raisins
1 lb. walnuts or pecans
½ lb. citron, chopped
1 lb. candied cherries

Sift flour, soda and spices together. Cream butter, add sugar gradually, and cream until fluffy. Add eggs and blend well. Add sifted dry ingredients and mix. Blend in combined milk and bourbon. Add remaining ingredients and mix well. Drop by spoonfuls on ungreased baking sheets. Bake in preheated 325° oven for 12 minutes. Makes about 10 dozen.

LEBKUCHEN

1½ c. light corn syrup
½ t. baking soda
¼ c. shortening
2 c. sifted flour
½ c. butter
1½ c. sugar
2 eggs
½ c. cultured sour cream
4½ c. sifted flour
¼ t. baking soda
1½ t. baking powder
½ t. cinnamon
⅛ t. cloves
1¼ t. salt
⅓ c. finely chopped blanched almonds
⅓ c. finely chopped citron
Blanched almonds

Combine syrup, ½ teaspoon soda and shortening; bring to a boil; remove from heat. Mix in 2 cups flour; cover; refrigerate for several days. Remove from refrigerator. Allow to come to room temperature. Cream butter; add sugar gradually; beat in eggs and sour cream. Mix in room-temperature syrup mixture. Stir in sifted dry ingredients, chopped almonds and citron. Cover; refrigerate for several days. Allow dough to soften at room temperature before rolling. Roll dough ¼ inch thick on floured surface. Cut in large oblong pieces about 3 x 2 inches or use cookie cutters. Place on greased cookie sheets; decorate with blanched almonds. Bake at 350° about 15 minutes or until delicately browned. Makes about 8 dozen, depending on size.

PRALINE STRIPS

24 whole graham crackers
1 c. butter
1 c. brown sugar, packed
1 c. chopped pecans

Arrange graham crackers in ungreased 15 x 10 x 1-inch pan. Place butter and sugar in saucepan. Heat to boiling point; boil 2 minutes. Stir in pecans; spread evenly over crackers. Bake at 350° about 10 minutes. Cut each cracker in half while warm. Makes 48.

PEANUT TOFFEE DIAMONDS

½ c. butter
½ c. chunk-style peanut butter
1 c. brown sugar, packed
1 egg
1 t. vanilla
¼ t. salt
2 c. sifted flour
1 c. chocolate bits, melted
½ c. chunk-style peanut butter
Whole salted peanuts

Cream butter and ½ cup peanut butter; add sugar gradually; beat in egg and vanilla. Blend in salt and flour. Pat into greased 15 x 10 x 1-inch pan. Bake at 325° for about 25 minutes. Combine chocolate and ½ cup peanut butter; spread over hot baked surface. Cut into diamonds while warm; place a peanut in center of each diamond. Makes about 4 dozen.

AUSTRIAN PEACH COOKIES

1 c. sugar
¾ c. vegetable oil
½ c. milk
2 eggs
¾ t. baking powder
½ t. vanilla
3½ to 4 c. flour
　Apricot filling
　Red and Yellow-Orange Sugars

In large bowl, combine sugar, oil, milk, eggs, baking powder and vanilla; blend in enough flour to form a soft dough. Roll into walnut-size balls and bake on ungreased cookie sheets for 15 to 20 minutes (cookies will be pale); cool completely. Scrape out cookies by gently rotating tip of sharp knife against flat side of cookie, leaving shell. Fill cookies with apricot filling. Press two cookies together to form a "peach." Brush lightly with additional brandy or water and immediately dip one spot in Red Sugar for blush, then roll entire cookie in Yellow-Orange Sugar for peach color. If desired, insert a piece of cinnamon stick "stem" through a green gumdrop "leaf" into the seam of each peach. Makes about 2½ dozen. Bake at 325°.

Apricot Filling

2 c. reserved cookie crumbs
1 c. peach or apricot preserves
½ c. chopped almonds
1 3-oz. package cream cheese, softened
2 T. instant tea powder
2 to 3 T. peach, apricot or plain brandy
¾ t. ground cinnamon

In medium bowl, combine ingredients. Mix until blended.

Red and Yellow-Orange Sugar

1 c. sugar
　Red food coloring
　Yellow food coloring

To make Red Sugar, blend ⅓ cup sugar with a few drops red food coloring. To make Yellow-Orange Sugar, blend ⅔ cup sugar with 2 to 3 drops red food coloring. Add enough yellow food coloring to make a peach color.

Austrian Peach Cookies

ORANGE WALNUT WAFERS

½ c. butter or margarine
1 c. brown sugar
1 egg
½ t. vanilla
1 T. grated orange rind
1¾ c. flour
½ t. baking soda
¼ t. salt
½ c. chopped walnuts

Beat together butter, sugar, egg, vanilla and orange rind. Combine flour, baking soda and salt; stir into butter mixture. Add walnuts and mix well. Form into rolls 2 inches in diameter. Wrap in waxed paper or plastic wrap. Chill. When firm, slice ⅛ inch thick. Place on ungreased cookie sheet and bake for 8 to 10 minutes at 400°.

LEMON REFRIGERATOR COOKIES

See photo, page 29

1½ c. sifted flour
½ t. baking soda
¾ t. salt
½ c. butter or margarine
1 c. sugar
1 egg
1 t. lemon juice
2 t. grated lemon rind

Sift together flour, soda and salt. Cream the butter, sugar, egg and lemon juice and rind. Beat until light. Gradually add dry ingredients, mixing well. Divide dough in half; tint one half pink if desired. Shape each half into a long smooth roll about 2 inches in diameter. Wrap rolls in aluminum foil. Chill or freeze until firm enough to slice easily. With sharp knife, slice cookies ⅛ inch thick. Place on ungreased, foil-covered cookie sheets. Bake at 400° for 6 to 8 minutes, until lightly browned. Makes about 5 dozen cookies.

LEMON BELLS

Make dough for Lemon Refrigerator Cookies. Shape about ½ cup of the dough into a long pencil-shaped roll and remaining dough into a large roll about 2 inches in diameter. Wrap both in foil and chill. Remove large roll from refrigerator and mold into a bell shape. Chill or freeze until needed. To bake, cut in ⅛-inch slices and arrange on foil-covered cookie sheet. Slice the tiny roll and place a small round at bottom of each cookie. Bake as above.

MELTAWAY MAPLE CRISPS

½ c. butter
¼ c. sugar
1 t. maple flavoring
2 c. sifted cake flour
¾ c. chopped pecans

Cream butter; add sugar gradually. Add flavoring and beat until fluffy. Stir in flour and mix until a dough forms. Fold in pecans and press into a ball. Pinch off small pieces of dough and place on ungreased cookie sheet. Flatten cookies with finger or glass dipped in sugar. Bake at 350° for 7 minutes.

CINNAMON STARS

3 egg whites
¼ t. salt
1½ c. confectioners' sugar
1 T. grated lemon rind
½ t. cinnamon
3 cups grated unblanched almonds

Beat egg whites and salt until stiff but not dry. Add powdered sugar gradually and blend thoroughly. Reserve ½ cup egg white mixture for topping. Add remaining ingredients; blend. Roll out dough, a small portion at a time, on a board that has been generously sprinkled with confectioners' sugar. Roll ¼ inch thick and cut with a small star cookie cutter. Place on a baking sheet that has been greased and covered with brown paper. Cover cookies with a thin layer of topping, spreading topping to the points of the stars. Bake for about 20 minutes at 300°. Remove from baking sheet immediately. If cookies stick, lift brown paper from baking sheet and place it on a moistened board. After about 1 minute, remove cookies from paper. Makes about 10 dozen.

HOLIDAY BON BONS

½ c. finely chopped walnuts
1 c. ground dates
½ t. vanilla
1 egg white
⅛ t. salt
⅓ c. sugar
½ t. vanilla
Red and green food coloring

Combine nuts, dates and vanilla. Form into balls, using a scant ½ teaspoon of the mixture for each. Refrigerate mixture thoroughly. Beat egg white and salt until stiff, adding sugar gradually. Add vanilla. Divide egg white mixture in half. Tint one portion pink and the other green. Use 1 or 2 teaspoons to roll balls in meringue. Swirl tops. Bake on greased cookie sheets in 250° oven for about ½ hour. Makes 4-5 dozen.

THIMBELINA COOKIES

½ c. butter, softened
¼ c. sugar
1 egg yolk, well beaten
1 t. vanilla

1 c. flour
½ t. salt
1 egg white, unbeaten
1 c. chopped walnuts

Cream together butter and sugar. Beat in egg yolk and vanilla. Blend in flour and salt, sifted together. Shape into 1-inch balls. Dip each ball into egg white; roll in nuts. Place on ungreased baking sheet. Dent center of each ball. Bake for 5 minutes at 350°. Remove from oven and dent again. Bake 12 to 15 additional minutes. Cool. Fill with Tinted Butter Frosting. Makes about 3 dozen.

TINTED BUTTER FROSTING

Combine 2 cups sifted confectioners' sugar, 6 tablespoons melted butter, 1 tablespoon cream and ½ teaspoon vanilla. Mix well. Tint with food coloring.

SWEDISH BUTTER COOKIES

1 c. butter
½ c. sugar
1 egg, separated
1 T. cream
1 t. vanilla
2 c. sifted flour
½ t. baking powder
½ c. chopped pecans

Cream butter and sugar. Add egg yolk, cream and vanilla and mix well. Sift flour with baking powder and add to butter mixture. Stir in nuts. Form dough into small balls and dip in egg white, then chopped pecans. Make a small indentation in the center of the balls of dough after placing them on an ungreased cookie sheet. Fill indentations with jelly or with a red or green maraschino cherry half. Bake at 350° for 20 minutes. Handle carefully when removing from cookie sheet as they are very fragile.

❄

HONEY LACE WAFERS

½ c. cake flour
¼ t. baking powder
⅛ t. baking soda
¼ c. honey
2 T. sugar
¼ c. butter
½ c. shredded coconut
1¾ t. grated orange rind (optional)

Sift flour once, measure, add baking powder and soda and sift again. Combine honey, sugar and butter in saucepan. Bring to a full boil and cook one minute. Remove from heat. Add sifted dry ingredients. Then add coconut and rind and mix well. Drop by ¼ teaspoonfuls onto greased and floured baking sheet. Bake a few at a time at 350° for 8-10 minutes. Let cool on sheet for about ½ minute; remove with spatula while still hot and immediately wrap cookies around a pencil, pressing edges together to seal. Makes about 3 dozen cookies.

PECAN FINGERS

1 c. butter
¼ c. confectioners' sugar
1 t. vanilla
1 T. water
2 c. flour
¼ t. salt
2 c. ground pecans
Confectioners' sugar

Cream butter; add sugar, vanilla and water. Beat well. Add flour and pecans. Chill for about 1 hour. Shape dough into small, fingerlike rolls. Bake for 1 hour at 250°. While cookies are still warm, roll them in confectioners' sugar. Makes about 5 dozen. *Note:* If you wish, form cookies into crescents, balls or other shapes. Always roll baked cookies in confectioners' sugar.

CRISP BUTTER WAFERS

1 c. butter   1 t. vanilla
⅔ c. sugar   1½ c. flour
1 egg   ¼ t. salt

Beat butter, sugar, egg and vanilla until fluffy. Add flour and salt and mix well. Drop from teaspoon onto ungreased cookie sheets. Bake at 350° for 8-10 minutes or until cookies begin to brown around the edges. Makes about 4 dozen.

ANISE DROPS

1¾ c. flour
½ t. baking powder
3 eggs
1 c. sugar
Anise oil

Sift flour and baking powder together; set aside. Combine eggs and sugar in large mixing bowl. Beat for 30 minutes on medium speed. Add flour; blend thoroughly. Beat for 3 additional minutes. Add anise oil to taste. Drop cookies from teaspoon onto greased baking sheets. Let stand overnight in a cool, dry place. Bake at 325° for about 12 minutes. Cookies should form a creamy white "cap." Makes 8-10 dozen cookies.

OLD-FASHIONED BROWNIES

2 oz. baking chocolate
½ c. shortening
1 c. sugar
2 eggs, well beaten
1 t. vanilla
½ c. sifted flour
¼ t. salt
½ c. chopped pecans

Melt chocolate and shortening in top part of double boiler over hot water. Remove from heat. Add sugar, eggs and vanilla. Mix well. Add flour and salt and mix well. Stir in nuts. Pour into greased 9 x 9-inch pan. Bake at 375° for 15 to 18 minutes. Cut into squares or bars.

CHOCOLATE MINT WAFERS

⅔ c. butter
1 c. sugar
1 egg
2 c. flour
¾ c. cocoa
½ t. salt
1 t. baking powder
¼ c. milk

Cream butter and sugar thoroughly. Add egg and beat well. Add sifted dry ingredients alternately with milk. Mix thoroughly; chill. Roll ⅛ inch thick on lightly floured surface. Cut with floured 2 to 2½ inch cookie cutter. Bake on greased sheet 350° for 8 minutes. When cool, put together with Mint Filling.

MINT FILLING

½ c. confectioners' sugar
2 drops peppermint oil
3 to 4 T. light cream or milk
Salt

Beat until of spreading consistency.

Gladys Eborall

PEANUT BUTTER REFRIGERATOR COOKIES

See photo opposite

2 c. sifted flour
1 t. baking soda
½ t. salt
1 c. soft butter or margarine
1 c. light brown sugar, firmly packed
1 c. chunk style peanut butter
1 egg
1 t. vanilla

Sift together flour, soda and salt. Cream the butter and sugar until light, then beat in peanut butter, egg and vanilla. Mix in the dry ingredients, blending thoroughly. Form the mixture into two long rolls, about 2 inches in diameter. Wrap in foil and chill or freeze until needed. To bake, slice cookies with a very sharp knife about ⅛ inch thick and place on an ungreased foil-covered cookie sheet. Bake at 375° about 6 to 8 minutes or until lightly browned. Makes about 8 dozen cookies.

Note: It's easy to form refrigerator cookies into holiday shapes. After making rolls of dough, gently press them into the desired shapes. Then chill as usual.

VANILLA REFRIGERATOR WAFERS

½ c. butter
½ c. margarine
1¼ c. confectioners' sugar
1 egg
1 t. vanilla
2 c. flour
1 t. baking soda
1 t. cream of tartar
⅛ t. salt

Cream together butter, margarine and sugar. Beat in egg and vanilla. Combine dry ingredients and add to creamed mixture. Mix well. Divide dough in half. Form each half into a roll 2 inches in diameter. Wrap in waxed paper or aluminum foil. Chill in refrigerator or freezer until ready to bake. Slice ⅜ inch thick. Bake on ungreased cookie sheet in 350° oven for 8 to 10 minutes. Cool on rack. Makes about 7 dozen.

CHERRY-COCONUT BARS

1 c. sifted flour
½ c. butter or margarine
3 T. confectioners' sugar
2 eggs, slightly beaten
1 c. sugar
¼ c. flour
½ t. baking powder
¼ t. salt
1 t. vanilla
¾ c. chopped nuts
½ c. coconut
½ c. quartered maraschino cherries

Mix butter, flour, and sugar until smooth. Spread thin with fingers in an 8 or 9-inch square pan. Bake at 350° about 25 minutes. Stir rest of ingredients into eggs. Spread over top of baked pastry. Bake about 25 minutes at 350°. Cool and cut into bars.

Pauline Follin

CHRISTMAS FRUIT BARS
See photo below

1¼ c. sifted flour
1½ t. baking powder
1 t. salt
3 eggs
1 c. sugar
1 t. vanilla
1½ c. chopped mixed candied fruits
½ c. chopped dates
1 c. chopped walnuts

Line two 8-inch square pans with aluminum foil and grease lightly. Sift together flour, baking powder and salt. Beat eggs until light; add sugar, a little at a time, beating after each addition. Add vanilla. Stir in dry ingredients. Fold in fruits and nuts. Spread dough in foil-lined pans. Bake at 350° for 25 to 30 minutes. Cool; cut into bars. Makes two 8-inch pans; 18 bars each pan.

Lemon Refrigerator Cookies, page 25   *Peanut Butter Refrigerator Cookies, opposite*   *Christmas Fruit Bars, this page*

CAKES

ALMOND CHIFFON CAKE

2 c. sifted all-purpose flour
1½ c. sugar
1 T. baking powder
1 t. salt
7 egg yolks
½ c. salad oil
1 t. lemon extract
1 t. almond extract
¾ c. ice water
7 egg whites (1 c.)
½ t. cream of tartar

Sift first 4 ingredients 4 times. Set aside. Combine egg yolks, salad oil, extracts and ice water. Add dry ingredients. Beat 30 seconds and set aside. Beat egg whites and cream of tartar until stiff peaks form (about 5 minutes). Gradually pour egg yolk mixture over beaten egg whites. Pour into ungreased 10" tube pan. Bake at 325° for 55 minutes, increase temperature to 350° and bake 10 minutes longer. Invert to cool for 1½-2 hours. Ice with Double Boiler Frosting.

DOUBLE BOILER FROSTING

2 egg whites
1½ c. sugar
¼ t. cream of tartar
⅓ c. water
1 t. vanilla

Combine egg whites, sugar, cream of tartar and water in top of double boiler. Beat on high for 1 minute with electric mixer. Place over boiling water and beat on high speed for 7 minutes. Remove pan from boiling water. Add vanilla. Beat 2 minutes longer on high speed. Spread on cake and sprinkle sliced almonds on top.

Geneva Bratton

HOLIDAY MINT ANGEL CAKE
See color photo opposite

8 egg whites (about 1 cup)
¼ t. salt
1 t. cream of tartar
1 t. almond extract
1 t. vanilla
1¼ c. granulated sugar
1 c. cake flour
3½ c. whipped topping
½ c. hard mint candies, coarsely crushed

Preheat oven to 325°. Place egg whites in a small mixing bowl and beat until foamy. Add salt and cream of tartar and beat until soft peaks form. Fold in almond extract and vanilla. Gradually beat in sugar and continue beating until stiff. Sift flour into egg whites and gently fold in. Bake in an ungreased 10-inch tube pan for 50 to 60 minutes. Invert pan on a rack or place center over a soft drink bottle. Cool thoroughly. Remove from pan and slice into 3 layers. Place layer on a cake plate. Drizzle about 2 tablespoons Mint Syrup over the bottom layer. Spread on ½ cup of the whipped topping. Sprinkle on about 1 tablespoon crushed mints. Add second layer and repeat above procedure. Invert the top layer and sprinkle with remaining syrup. Place right side up on second layer. Spread entire cake with remaining whipped topping. Sprinkle with remaining crushed mints. If desired, place scoops of vanilla ice cream on top. Place in freezer until ready to serve.

MINT SYRUP

¼ c. hard mint candies
¼ c. water

Place mints in a blender and blend at high speed until coarsely crushed. Add water and blend until thick.

POPPY SEED CAKE

½ c. shortening
1½ c. sugar
⅔ c. poppy seeds
¼ t. salt
1¼ c. milk
1 t. almond extract
2 c. flour
3 egg whites
3½ t. baking powder

Cream shortening and sugar well. Add poppy seeds and mix thoroughly. Sift flour, salt and baking powder in separate bowl. Add dry ingredients and milk alternately, making sure to combine thoroughly after each addition. Add almond extract. Beat egg whites until perfect peaks form. Then fold into batter. Bake at 360° in 2 greased and floured layer cake pans (or a bundt pan) for 25 to 30 minutes, or until done. Cool completely and ice.

CREAM CHEESE ICING

1 3-oz. package cream cheese
1 T. milk
2½ c. confectioners' sugar
½ T. vanilla

Soften cheese with milk; add sugar and vanilla. Mix until smooth. If making a 2-layer cake, ice just center and top. If using a bundt pan ice the cake completely.

Patricia Dodson

APRICOT MINI SEVEN-LAYER CAKES

1 11¾-oz. package frozen pound cake
1 16-oz. can apricot halves, undrained
1 t. grated lemon peel
1 16½-oz. can vanilla frosting
2 T. minced maraschino cherries, well drained on paper towels
1 oz. semisweet chocolate, melted
¼ c. smooth peanut butter

Cut frozen cake in 21 vertical slices using a serrated knife with a sawing motion; set aside. Reserve 6 of the apricot halves for garnishing top of cakes. Whirl remaining undrained apricots and lemon peel in a blender until smooth. Spread some of the pureed apricots on a cake slice to within ⅛ inch of edge. Top with a second slice. Continue layering to make 7-layer "mini" cake. Place cake on its side on a serving platter with remaining cake slices until you have three separate "mini" cakes. Divide frosting into three small bowls. Stir cherries into one bowl, stir chocolate into second bowl, stir peanut butter into third bowl. If frostings thicken, thin to spreading consistency with a few drops of milk. Spread the sides and top of each cake with a different flavored frosting. Cut reserved apricots into slices. Decorate top of each cake with apricot slices. Chill until ready to serve.

EASY CHOCOLATE CAKE

½ c. butter or margarine
1¼ c. sugar
2 oz. unsweetened chocolate
2 eggs
½ t. baking powder
2 c. sifted flour
1 c. cold water
1 t. baking soda
¼ t. salt
1 t. vanilla
1 6-oz. package semisweet chocolate bits

Cream butter and sugar; add melted chocolate and beat thoroughly. Add well-beaten eggs. Sift baking powder, flour and salt together; add to mixture alternately with soda and water combined, beating well after each addition. Add vanilla and pour into greased baking pan, 9 x 13 inches. Sprinkle chocolate bits evenly over batter. Bake at 350° for 20 minutes or until done. Cool. Sprinkle with confectioners' sugar if desired.

Millicent Sprtel

VANILLA WAFER CAKE

¾ c. margarine
1½ c. sugar
6 eggs
3 c. vanilla wafer crumbs
½ c. milk
1 c. chopped pecans
1⅓ c. flaked coconut

Cream margarine. Gradually add sugar; cream until light and fluffy. Add eggs one at a time. Beat well after each addition. Alternately fold in crumbs and milk. Stir in nuts and coconut. Batter may appear curdled. Spoon into 9-inch tube pan which has been greased, floured and lined on bottom with waxed paper. Evenly spread batter in pan. Bake at 350° for 1 hour 10 minutes. Cool cake in pan 10 minutes; remove from pan; remove waxed paper and finish cooling on rack. Frost or glaze as desired.

Estella Long Black

MORAVIAN SUGAR CAKE

6 T. melted margarine
½ c. seasoned mashed potatoes
½ c. sugar
1 pkg. dry yeast
1 egg
½ t. salt
2½ c. flour

Dissolve yeast in ½ cup warm water for 5 minutes. Beat all ingredients well with an electric mixer except 1 cup of the flour. Then add the 1 cup of flour and mix with a spoon. Put dough into a greased bowl and let rise 2 hours or until double in bulk (it can be put in an 85° oven to rise). Punch down and spread in a 9 x 13-inch pan. Let rise ½ hour.

Sift ½ cup brown sugar and ½ teaspoon cinnamon. Make about 24 holes with little pats of cold margarine in the dough. Sprinkle with sugar and cinnamon mixture. Bake about 20 minutes at 400°.

Mrs. Edward L. Fischer

APPLESAUCE CAKE

1 c. brown sugar
1 c. white sugar
1 c. butter or margarine
2 eggs
3 c. flour
½ t. salt
1½ t. baking soda
1 t. cloves
1 t. nutmeg
1 t. cinnamon
1 c. applesauce
1 c. chocolate chips
½ c. raisins
1 c. coconut
1 c. chopped pecans

Blend together sugars and butter; add eggs. Combine flour with spices, salt and soda. Mix well and add to sugar and egg mixture. Add applesauce, chocolate chips, raisins, coconut and pecans. Pour into a 10-inch tube pan which has been lined with brown paper. Bake at 350° for 1½ hours. If cake browns too quickly, cover with an extra piece of brown paper. Keeps well.

Alice Leedy Mason

NUT DELIGHT CAKE

3 c. flour
2 c. sugar
1½ c. salad oil
1 t. vanilla
4 eggs, beaten
½ t. salt
1½ t. baking soda
1 large can evaporated milk
½ c. raisins (optional)
½ c. chopped walnuts
1 can nut filling

Combine all ingredients except nut filling. Beat until smooth. Add nut filling and beat at medium speed for about 3 minutes. Bake at 350° for about 1 hour and 10 minutes in an ungreased tube pan. Cool cake for at least ½ hour before removing from pan. Cake can be eaten same day, but its flavor improves with age.

Doris K. Finck

MINI-FRUITCAKES
See color photo opposite

3 c. unsifted flour
1⅓ c. sugar
1 t. salt
1 t. baking powder
2 t. ground cinnamon
1 t. ground nutmeg
½ c. orange juice
½ c. brandy or water
1 c. salad oil
4 eggs
¼ c. light corn syrup
1 c. dark seedless raisins
2 c. diced dried California apricots
2 c. mixed candied fruits (1 lb.)
2 c. pecan halves
⅓ c. light corn syrup

In large mixing bowl, combine all ingredients except fruits, nuts, and ⅓ cup corn syrup. Blend for ½ minute on low speed, scraping bowl constantly. Beat 3 minutes on high speed, scraping bowl occasionally. Stir in fruits and nuts. Spoon batter into 3 dozen 2½-inch muffin pans lined with paper baking cups. Bake in 275° oven for 65 to 70 minutes or until toothpick comes out clean when inserted in center of fruitcake. Cool fruitcakes in pans for 5 minutes; remove to cooling rack. Cool thoroughly. Heat corn syrup in small pan; brush over tops of cakes. Place cupcakes in container; cover with cheesecloth soaked in brandy. Cover tightly and store in a cool place for up to 2 weeks. For longer storage, freeze in tightly covered containers. Makes about 3 dozen.

CHEESECAKE

¾ stick butter, melted
9 whole graham crackers
2 T. sugar

Mix together and press in greased 9-inch round pan lined with aluminum foil.

CHEESE FILLING

3 8-oz. packages cream cheese
¾ c. sugar
3 eggs
Pinch of salt

Mix above ingredients and pour into crust. Bake 20 minutes at 375°.

SOUR CREAM TOPPING

1 pt. sour cream
1 T. sugar
1 t. vanilla

Mix and pour on top of pie. Bake 5 minutes at 475°. Cool in refrigerator several hours before serving.

Jackie Gray

POUND CAKE DELIGHT

½ c. shortening
1 c. butter
3 c. sugar
1 c. sweet milk
3½ c. sifted flour
6 eggs
1 t. baking powder
½ t. salt
1 t. rum extract
1 t. coconut extract
1 t. lemon extract

Cream the first 3 ingredients. Add eggs one at a time. Add sifted dry ingredients alternately with milk and flavorings. Bake at 325° for 1 hour 20 minutes to 1 hour 30 minutes in 10-inch greased and floured tube pan.

ALMOND ICING

1 c. sugar
½ c. water
1 t. almond extract

Boil ingredients together for about 2 minutes. Pour over warm cake which has been poked with holes with a meat fork.

Geneva Bratton

Photo opposite
Mini-Fruitcakes, this page
Brandied Apricots, page 52
Apricot Snowballs, page 6

DECORATING, GLAZING AND STORING FRUITCAKES

Let baked fruitcakes stand in pans until almost cold. Remove from pans; cool on racks until the following day. Cover loosely with clean towels.

Wrap cold fruitcakes in 2 thicknesses of waxed paper and store in a tightly covered container. Or wrap in a cloth moistened with wine or brandy, or pour about ¼ cup wine or brandy over each cake. Then wrap cakes in waxed paper and place in a tightly covered container; moisten the cloth or pour liquor over cakes 2 or 3 times during aging period.

To make Apricot Glaze, force 1 cup stewed or canned apricots through a fine sieve. Add ¾ cup sugar and ⅓ cup boiling water; cook uncovered until mixture is as thick as jam. Cool.

Allow fruitcakes to ripen for several weeks before glazing or serving. Then arrange nuts and candied fruits on cakes in the designs desired. Cover fruit-cakes and decorations with Apricot Glaze. Before packing or serving cakes, let glaze dry for several hours.

DARK FRUITCAKE

1 c. light molasses	2¼ c. sifted flour
½ c. water	¼ t. baking soda
2 lbs. seedless raisins	1 t. salt
2 lbs. mixed candied fruit, diced	1½ t. cinnamon
	1¼ t. nutmeg
1 c. butter	¾ t. allspice
1¼ c. sugar	½ t. cloves
6 eggs	½ c. orange juice
1 T. grated orange rind	3 c. coarsely chopped nuts

Blend molasses and water together in a large saucepan. Bring to a boil at a medium heat; stir constantly. Add raisins; bring to a boil again; stir well. Reduce heat to low; simmer for 5 minutes. Remove from heat; mix in candied fruit; set aside to cool. Cream butter; add sugar gradually; beat in eggs one at a time; add orange rind. Add sifted dry ingredients alternately with orange juice to creamed mixture. Stir in fruit mixture and nuts. Pour into 2 greased 9 x 5 x 3-inch pans lined with waxed paper; grease paper. Bake in 275° oven for about 3 hours. Makes two 3½-pound fruitcakes.

WHITE FRUITCAKE

1 c. butter or margarine
1 c. sugar
2 c. flour (more if needed)
5 eggs
2 t. baking powder
½ t. salt
1 lb. pecans or walnuts
1 lb. white raisins
1 lb. fruit mix
½ lb. coconut
1 small can crushed pineapple
1 12-oz. jar maraschino cherries, drained (optional)
1 12-oz. package dried apricots (optional)

Cream the butter or margarine; add the sugar and mix. Beat in eggs. Sift dry ingredients together; add to creamed mixture alternately with fruit. Mix all very thoroughly. The mixture will be thick but do not add any additional liquid. Spoon into small baking tins and bake for ½ hour at 275°, then 1 hour at 300°. Makes 3 small cakes.

Barbara T. Price

NO-BAKE HOLIDAY FRUITCAKE

1 qt. paperboard milk carton, empty
4 c. pound cake crumbs (11¼-oz. cake)
1½ c. miniature marshmallows
1¼ c. cut-up mixed candied fruits
1 c. seedless raisins
¾ c. finely cut dates
¾ c. chopped walnuts
½ t. cinnamon
½ t. nutmeg
¼ t. cloves
⅓ c. milk
2 T. frozen orange juice concentrate, undiluted

Rinse out milk carton and let dry. Cut out one side of carton (see photo); set carton on side to form a pan and place cut-out piece in bottom of pan to make a sliding base for cake. Flatten pouring end of carton and secure with tape. Break pound cake into crumbs by hand or in blender. In large bowl combine pound cake crumbs with marshmallows, fruits, nuts and spices. Add milk and orange juice concentrate; mix with spoon, then with hands until crumbs are evenly moistened. Pack into prepared milk carton. If desired, garnish with additional fruits and nuts. Cover with plastic wrap and chill at least 2 days before slicing. Makes one 2-pound fruitcake.

Note: For 4-pound fruitcake, double above recipe and pack into ½-gallon milk carton. During chilling, turn carton on its side with weight on top to keep sides of cake straight. For two 1-pound fruitcakes, pack half of above mixture into each of two 1-pint milk cartons. For four ½-pound fruitcakes, pack ¼ of above mixture into each of four ½-pint milk cartons. To prepare ½-pint cartons, cut off entire top to make a square container.

BREADS AND COFFEE CAKES

CHRISTMAS APRICOT WREATH
See color photo opposite

1 13¾-oz. package hot roll mix
¼ c. butter or margarine, softened
1 egg, beaten
    Fruit-Nut Filling
    Confectioners' Sugar Glaze
6 dried California apricots

Prepare hot roll mix according to directions; allow to rise for 35 minutes or until doubled in bulk. Roll out dough to an 18 x 15-inch rectangle. Spread with butter. Sprinkle Fruit-Nut Filling evenly over dough. Roll up, jelly roll fashion, starting with the long end. Place dough on ungreased baking sheet; form into a wreath. Allow to rise about 30 minutes. Brush ring with beaten egg. Bake in 325° oven 35 to 40 minutes or until lightly browned. Cool on sheet for 5 minutes. Loosen bottom of coffee cake with a long metal spatula. Carefully remove to rack. Cool to lukewarm. Drizzle glaze over surface of warm coffee cake. To garnish, form "flowers" by arranging apricot halves in ring around top of coffee cake. Cut red cherries reserved from filling into halves; place one in the center of each apricot flower. Cut each reserved green cherry into 5 wedges and use to garnish apricot flowers.

FRUIT-NUT FILLING

1 4-oz. jar red glacé cherries
1 4-oz. jar green glacé cherries
1 c. diced dried California apricots
⅔ c. chopped toasted blanched almonds
¼ c. sugar
2 T. brandy

Set 3 red and 6 green cherries aside for garnish; chop remaining cherries. Combine all ingredients in bowl. Mix together thoroughly.

CONFECTIONERS' SUGAR GLAZE

1 c. confectioners' sugar
4 t. milk
1 T. brandy

Stir ingredients together in a small bowl until well mixed and of spreading consistency.

Note: Coffee cake may be prepared, completely baked, then frozen until serving day. Instead of glazing cooled cake, wrap in foil and freeze. To serve, thaw in foil at room temperature for 3 hours, then heat for 20 minutes in 300° oven. Glaze as directed.

APRICOT-CRANBERRY LOAF
See color photo opposite

2 c. unsifted flour
¾ c. sugar
1 T. baking powder
½ t. salt
1 c. diced dried California apricots
1 c. chopped fresh or frozen cranberries
½ c. chopped toasted almonds
2 eggs
1 c. milk
¼ c. butter or margarine, melted
1 t. grated lemon peel

Stir flour, sugar, baking powder and salt together in large bowl; add apricots, cranberries and almonds. Toss lightly until fruits are coated. Beat eggs, milk, butter and peel in small bowl; pour over dry ingredients. Stir just until dry ingredients are moistened. Pour into a greased 9 x 5-inch loaf pan. Bake at 350° for 60 to 65 minutes or until cake tester inserted in center comes out clean. Cool in pan for 10 minutes; finish cooling on rack. Makes 1 loaf.

Photo opposite
Apricot-Cranberry Loaf, this page
Christmas Apricot Wreath, this page
Apricot Sticky Buns, page 45

RUSSIAN KULICH

See photo opposite

5 c. flour
2 packages dry yeast
1 c. milk
½ c. sugar
¼ c. vegetable oil
2 t. salt
2 eggs
2 t. grated lemon peel
½ c. chopped blanched almonds
¼ c. raisins
¼ c. chopped candied citron
¼ c. chopped candied orange peel
¼ c. chopped candied cherries
½ c. confectioners' sugar
1 T. milk
   Candied fruit (optional)

Stir together 1 cup flour and yeast. Heat 1 cup milk, sugar, oil and salt over low heat to 120° to 130°, stirring to blend. Add to flour-yeast mixture; beat until smooth, about 2 minutes on medium speed of mixer. Beat in eggs, lemon peel, almonds, raisins and candied fruit. Add 1 cup flour; beat 1 minute on medium speed. Stir in more flour to make a soft dough. Turn out onto lightly floured board or pastry cloth; knead until smooth and satiny, about 8 to 10 minutes. Shape into ball and place in lightly greased bowl; turn to grease surface of ball. Cover; let rise in warm place (80 to 85°) until doubled, about 1½ hours. Punch down. Divide dough into 2 or 3 equal portions and shape into balls. Let rest 10 minutes. Generously grease two 46-ounce juice cans or three 1-pound coffee cans. Place dough in cans, filling about half full; brush with oil. Let rise until doubled, about 1 hour. Bake in preheated 350° oven for 30 to 35 minutes or until golden brown. Immediately remove from cans and cool. Blend confectioners' sugar and 1 tablespoon milk until smooth; ice top of loaves. Decorate with candied fruit if desired. 3 medium or 2 large loaves.

KUGELHUPF

See photo opposite

3 to 4 c. flour
2 packages dry yeast
1 c. milk
1 c. raisins
½ c. water
½ c. sugar
½ c. butter
1 t. salt
3 eggs, room temperature
2 t. rum extract
   Butter, softened
⅓ c. ground almonds
   Sifted confectioners' sugar
   Candied fruits
   Nuts
   Light corn syrup

Stir together 2 cups flour and yeast. Heat milk, raisins, water, sugar, ½ cup butter and salt over low heat to 120° to 130°, stirring to blend; add to flour-yeast mixture and beat until smooth, about 3 minutes on medium speed of mixer. Blend in eggs and extract; add ½ cup flour and continue to beat 2 minutes. Add enough flour to make a thick batter. Cover; let rise in a warm place (80 to 85°) until doubled in volume and batter is bubbly, about 1 hour. Stir down. Spoon into two 1½-quarts or three 1-quart ram's head or other fancy molds that have been buttered and dusted with ground almonds. Cover; let rise in warm place until doubled, about 30 minutes. Bake in preheated 325° oven 1 hour for 1½-quart loaves or 45 minutes for 1-quart loaves. If necessary to prevent excessive browning, cover during the last 10 minutes of baking. Unmold on wire racks. Dust with confectioners' sugar. Decorate with candied fruits and nuts that have been dipped in corn syrup. 2 large or 3 small loaves.

BANANA-NUT BREAD

2 eggs
2 c. brown sugar
2 c. sour milk or buttermilk
1 t. baking soda
1 t. baking powder
3 c. sifted flour
1 c. wheat germ
1 t. salt
1 c. nuts
1 c. mashed bananas

Beat eggs until light. Add sugar and beat slightly. Add milk. Sift together flour, soda, baking powder and salt and add to eggs and sugar. Then add wheat germ, nuts and bananas. Bake in two loaves at 350° for 1 hour.

Ginny Muente

Russian Kulich, opposite
Kugelhupf, opposite
Austrian Almond Braid, this page

AUSTRIAN ALMOND BRAID
See photo at left

5 to 5½ c. flour
2 packages dry yeast
1 c. milk
½ c. sugar
½ c. shortening or butter
¼ c. water
2 t. salt
2 eggs, room temperature
½ c. golden raisins
½ c. candied mixed fruit, chopped
½ c. chopped blanched almonds
 Vegetable oil
 Almond Icing

Stir together 2 cups flour and yeast. Heat milk, sugar, shortening, water and salt in saucepan over low heat to 120° to 130°, stirring to blend. Add liquid ingredients to flour-yeast mixture and beat until smooth, about 3 minutes on medium speed of mixer. Blend in eggs. Add 1 cup flour and beat 1 minute. Stir in fruit and almonds; add more flour to make a soft dough. Turn out on lightly floured board and knead until smooth and satiny, about 5 to 10 minutes. Cover dough; let rest 20 minutes. Divide dough in half. For each braid, take two-thirds of 1 portion of dough and divide into thirds. Roll each piece with hands into a 15-inch strand. Braid strands on lightly greased baking sheet. Divide remaining third into thirds; form three 18-inch strands. Braid strands loosely; place on first braid, pressing in lightly. Tuck ends of top braid under ends of bottom braid. Brush with oil and let rise in warm place (80 to 85°) until doubled, about 45 minutes. Bake in preheated 350° oven for 25 to 30 minutes, or until golden brown. Remove from baking sheets to cooling rack. Ice braids with Almond Icing while still slightly warm. Decorate with candied fruit and nuts, if desired. 2 large loaves.

ALMOND ICING

1½ c. confectioners' sugar
2 T. milk
1 t. almond extract

In small bowl, stir together all ingredients until smooth.

DATE & NUT LOAF

1¾ c. whole nuts
13 oz. whole dates
¾ c. flour
2 t. baking powder
2 eggs, separated
½ c. sugar
1 t. vanilla

Mix together all ingredients except egg whites. Fold in stiffly beaten egg whites last. Batter will be stiff. Press into loaf pan. Bake at 325° for 1 hour. Cool before slicing.

Hazel I. Dalton

CHEESE BISCUITS

½ lb. sharp cheese
½ c. butter
1 c. flour
¼ t. red pepper
¼ t. salt

All ingredients should be at room temperature. Grate cheese into a large bowl. Add remaining ingredients and blend thoroughly. Roll out ⅓ to ½ inch thick. Cut in small rounds. Place on ungreased baking sheet and brush tops with milk. Bake at 400° until lightly browned.

APRICOT CAROLING TREE
See color photo opposite

1 13¾-oz. package hot roll mix
¼ c. butter or margarine, softened
9 jumbo green gumdrops, cut in halves crosswise
18 whole candied red cherries
6 canned apricot halves, well drained
6 small green birthday candles
Apricot Filling

Prepare hot roll mix according to package directions for rolls. Cover; let rise in warm place, free from draft, until doubled in bulk, about 30 to 45 minutes. Turn dough onto floured surface and knead lightly until not sticky. Roll dough into a 16 x 12-inch rectangle; spread with butter. Spread cooled filling evenly on dough to within ½ inch of edges. Starting with 16-inch side, roll up jelly roll fashion; seal edges. Cut into sixteen 1-inch slices. Grease a large (17 x 14-inch) baking sheet. Using a spatula, arrange the 16 slices, cut side down, in a triangle shape in 5 rows. For first row, place 1 slice at top of 14-inch side of cookie sheet. Increase by 1 slice for each additional row, with slices touching; last row will contain 5 slices. Place remaining slice under last row to form base of Christmas tree. Cover; let rise in warm place, free from drafts, until doubled in bulk, about 30 to 45 minutes. Bake at 375° for 20 to 25 minutes or until lightly browned. Carefully remove from baking sheet to cool on wire rack. To decorate tree, make 6 apricot cluster flowers: arrange 3 gumdrop halves, cut side up, alternately with 3 whole cherries in a 3-inch circle. Top with well-drained apricot half, cut side down. Place candle in center of apricot. Decorate tree by arranging 3 apricot clusters in a row near the bottom, 2 in the middle and 1 near the top of tree.

APRICOT FILLING

1 16- or 17-oz. can apricot halves, drained
¾ c. apricot preserves
3 T. cornstarch
1½ t. grated orange peel
½ c. chopped walnuts

Cut each apricot into quarters. In a medium saucepan, combine apricots, preserves, cornstarch and orange peel. Cook over medium heat, stirring constantly, until mixture thickens and begins to boil. Cover and chill until cool; stir in walnuts.

Photo opposite
Apricot Caroling Tree, this page
Apricot Calico Cookies, page 20

PANETONE

2 packages dry yeast
4¼ to 4¾ c. all-purpose flour
½ c. milk, scalded
½ c. warm water (110°-115°)
1½ t. anise seed
¼ c. soft butter
½ c. sugar
1 t. salt
2 eggs, room temperature
¾ t. vanilla
⅓ c. cut-up candied fruit
½ c. chopped nuts
2 T. pine nuts, if desired
½ c. raisins, dark or golden
1 egg, beaten
1 T. water

Stir yeast into 1½ cups flour in large mixing bowl. Measure milk, water, anise seed, butter, sugar and salt into a saucepan. Heat until warm (120°-130°), stirring constantly.

Pour into bowl. Add eggs and vanilla. Beat ½ minute at low speed, scraping bowl constantly. Beat 3 more minutes at high speed. Add candied fruit, nuts and raisins. Gradually add enough additional flour to form a soft dough. Turn onto lightly floured board. Knead until smooth. Place dough in greased bowl. Turn over. Cover. Let rise on a rack over hot water for 1 to 1½ hours, until doubled and a dent is left when finger is pressed deep into side of dough. Punch down dough. Let rest 10 minutes. Divide dough into 2 pieces and shape each into a ball. Place on opposite corners of a large greased baking sheet. Flatten tops of balls slightly with knuckles. Let loaves rise again until doubled, 45 to 60 minutes. Just before baking, brush loaves with 1 beaten egg mixed with 1 tablespoon water. Bake in preheated 375° oven 30 to 40 minutes or until well browned. Remove from pan; cool on racks. Makes 2 loaves.

APRICOT STICKY BUNS
See color photo, page 39

1 13¾-oz. package hot roll mix
½ c. finely diced dried apricots
¼ c. water
¼ c. sugar
2 T. butter or margarine, softened
¼ c. blanched almonds
   Confectioners' Sugar Glaze (optional)

Prepare hot roll mix according to package directions; let rise as directed. While dough is rising, combine dried apricots, water and sugar in saucepan. Bring to a boil and simmer for 15 minutes, uncovered, until most of liquid has evaporated and apricots are tender. Remove from heat and stir in butter and chopped almonds. Set aside to cool. Punch dough down and roll out on lightly floured board to form a 12 x 10-inch rectangle. Spread dough with cooled apricot mixture. Beginning at long side, roll up jelly roll fashion. Seal edge tightly. Cut into 12 rolls, each 1 inch thick. Transfer to well-greased muffin tins. Cover and let rise until a finger pushed into the dough leaves a dent. Bake at 350° for 30 minutes or until browned. Remove from pan immediately. If desired, drizzle Confectioners' Sugar Glaze over warm buns.

CONFECTIONERS' SUGAR GLAZE

1 T. butter or margarine, softened
1 c. confectioners' sugar
3 T. milk

Combine ingredients and blend thoroughly.

RAISIN BREAD

2 c. raisins	1½ c. sugar
2 c. water	Dash of salt
2 t. baking soda	1½ t. vanilla
2 eggs	3 c. flour
1 c. nutmeats	

Combine raisins, water and soda; bring to a boil. Cool completely. Beat together eggs, sugar, salt and vanilla. Add raisin mixture with flour and eggs. Fold in nuts. Bake at 350° for 1 hour.

Gladys Daniels

Make your favorite sweet bread dough into a special holiday treat by forming it into a star, wreath or cane shape. If you feel particularly ambitious, try shaping an angel or Christmas tree. Decorate with colored icing.

Yeast breads usually have the best flavor the day they are baked, so make them as close to the gift day as possible.

Stiff raised breads can be baked on cookie sheets instead of in pans. This allows more variety in shaping the bread. For a rich golden crust, brush with an egg wash made by lightly beating together one egg yolk and a tablespoon of water.

Give a loaf of homemade bread on a breadboard. Wrap it in clear plastic, decorate with ribbon and a sprig of evergreen.

Make breads in fancy shapes by baking them in cans, molds or other unusual containers. Let your imagination be your guide. You can use any oven-proof container that is open on the top so the bread has room to rise.

MARMALADE-NUT BREAD

2½ c. unsifted flour, stirred before measuring
⅓ c. sugar
3½ t. baking powder
1 t. salt
1 c. coarsely chopped walnuts
1 egg
1 c. sweet orange marmalade
1 c. orange juice
3 T. vegetable oil

In large mixing bowl, thoroughly stir together flour, sugar, baking powder and salt.

Add walnuts; toss to coat evenly. In medium bowl, beat egg slightly; stir in marmalade, orange juice and vegetable oil. Add to flour mixture; stir only until dry ingredients are moistened. Divide batter evenly between 2 well-greased loaf pans, 8½ x 4½ x 2½-inches. Bake in preheated 350° oven 1 hour or until wooden pick inserted in center comes out clean. Cool in pans on rack 10 minutes; remove from pans; cool thoroughly on rack. Wrap tightly in foil. Allow flavors to mellow overnight before serving.

STOLLEN

2 packages active dry yeast
¼ c. warm water
1½ c. milk
½ c. sugar
1½ t. salt
¾ c. butter
2 c. sifted flour
3 eggs, beaten
½ t. ground cardamom
½ c. seedless raisins
1 c. sliced candied red and green cherries
4 c. sifted flour (about)
Melted butter

Soften active dry yeast in warm water. Scald milk; stir in sugar, salt and butter; cool to lukewarm. Mix in 2 cups flour, yeast, eggs, cardamom and fruit. Add enough remaining flour to make a stiff dough. Knead on floured surface; place in greased bowl; grease top of dough; cover. Let rise until doubled. Punch dough down; cover; let rest 10 minutes. Divide into three equal parts. Shape each piece into a 10 x 8-inch oval; fold lengthwise. Place in greased shallow pans. Let rise until almost doubled. Bake at 350° about 30 minutes. Frost and decorate if desired. Makes 3 stollen.

DANISH COFFEE CAKE

2 c. sugar
1 T. cinnamon
1 c. shortening
4 eggs, separated
¼ t. salt
3 c. flour
3 t. baking powder
1 c. milk
1 t. vanilla or almond extract

Make a mixture of ½ cup sugar and cinnamon. Mix well and set aside. Cream shortening, gradually add 1½ cups sugar and cream well. Add the egg yolks singly and beat. Combine flour and baking powder; add to creamed mixture alternately with milk. Combine salt and egg whites and beat until stiff. Add flavoring and mix well. Then fold the 2 mixtures together. Spoon layers of batter into a well-oiled bundt pan, with cinnamon mixture on top of each layer of batter. Try to use all the cinnamon mixture. Bake 1 hour in a 375° oven. Let cool 10 minutes. Loosen sides with a knife and turn out on rack to cool completely. Sift confectioners' sugar over top and sides of cake.

Edna M. Wagner

HONEY WHEAT BREAD

1 package dry yeast
1 c. warm water
½ c. honey
1 T. salt
2 T. shortening
1 c. milk, scalded
3 c. whole wheat flour
3 c. white flour

Dissolve yeast in warm water. Combine honey, salt, shortening and hot milk; stir until shortening melts. Cool to lukewarm. Add yeast mixture. Gradually add flours. Knead until satiny, 8-10 minutes. Place in greased bowl; cover. Let rise in warm place for 2-2½ hours. Punch down; let rise again. Shape into 2 loaves. Put in greased pans, 9 x 5 inches. Let rise until tops of loaves are above pan edges. Bake at 350° for 50 to 60 minutes.

SAFFRON BREAD

2½ c. milk
½ lb. butter
1 package saffron
1 t. salt
2 oz. yeast
1 c. sugar
2 eggs
8 c. flour
1½ c. seeded raisins

Heat milk, add butter to melt and cool to lukewarm. Dissolve saffron and yeast in 1 teaspoon milk. Add to milk—blend in beaten eggs. Stir in flour until sticky and knead in rest of flour along with raisins. Keep kneading until smooth, firm and glossy. Let rise in greased bowl until double in size. Place on board and shape into braided loaves. Let rise 1 hour after placing in bread tins. Bake at 375° for 45 minutes. Makes 2 loaves.

Jill Susan Dalbey

Mexican Fiesta Bread

MEXICAN FIESTA BREAD

4½ to 5½ c. flour
 2 packages dry yeast
⅔ c. milk
½ c. water
½ c. butter
⅓ c. sugar
 1 t. salt
 3 eggs, room temperature
 1 c. candied fruit
 1 c. chopped nuts
   Vegetable oil
   Powdered Sugar Frosting
   Candied fruit or nuts

Stir together 1¾ cups flour and yeast. Heat milk, water, butter, sugar and salt over low heat to 120 to 130°, stirring to blend. Add liquid ingredients to flour-yeast mixture and beat until smooth, about 3 minutes on medium speed of mixer. Blend in eggs. Add 1 cup flour and beat 1 minute on medium speed. Stir in fruit, nuts and more flour to make a moderately soft dough. (Dough will be sticky.) Turn onto lightly floured surface and knead until smooth and satiny, about 5 to 10 minutes. Cover dough; let rest 20 minutes. Roll into 22 x 12-inch rectangle. Roll up jelly roll fashion, starting at 22-inch end. Seal bottom; pinch ends together to form a ring. Place seam down in greased 10-inch tube pan. Brush with oil; let rise in warm place (80 to 85°) until doubled, about 1 hour. Bake in preheated 375° oven 50 to 60 minutes, or until done. Remove from pan immediately. Cool. Frost with Confectioners' Sugar Frosting; decorate with candied fruit or nuts. One 10-inch tube.

CONFECTIONERS' SUGAR FROSTING

1 c. confectioners' sugar, sifted
5 t. milk

Blend together sugar and milk.

QUICK COFFEE CAKE

¼ c. shortening
½ c. sugar
 1 egg
½ c. milk
1½ c. flour
1½ t. baking powder
½ t. nutmeg
½ t. salt
½ t. vanilla

Beat egg slightly; add shortening, and sugar and mix well. Stir in milk. Sift together flour, baking powder, nutmeg and salt. Add to egg mixture. Stir in vanilla. Pour into greased and floured 9-inch square pan. Sprinkle with Brown Sugar Topping. Bake at 375° for 25-30 minutes.

BROWN SUGAR TOPPING

½ c. brown sugar
1½ T. butter, melted
 1 T. flour
½ t. cinnamon

Combine ingredients until well blended.

HUNGARIAN CHRISTMAS BREAD

4½ to 5 c. flour
2 packages dry yeast
½ c. milk
½ c. water
½ c. sugar
¼ c. oil
2 t. salt
2 eggs
1 12-oz. can poppy-seed cake and pastry filling
1 c. golden raisins
1 egg, room temperature
Poppy seeds

Stir together 2 cups flour and yeast. Heat milk, water, sugar, oil and salt over low heat to 120° to 130°, stirring to blend. Add liquid ingredients to flour mixture and beat until smooth, about 2 minutes on medium speed of electric mixer. Blend in 2 eggs. Add 1 cup flour and beat 1 minute. Stir in enough additional flour to make a moderately stiff dough. Turn onto lightly floured board and knead until smooth and satiny, 5 to 8 minutes. Cover with pan or bowl; let rest 30 minutes. Divide in half. Roll each half into 10 x 12-inch rectangle. Spread with poppy-seed filling, leaving 1-inch margin on all sides; sprinkle with raisins. Roll up jelly roll fashion. Seal bottom and ends securely. Place on greased baking sheet, seam side down. Make shallow, diagonal cuts across top. Beat egg; brush tops and side of dough. Sprinkle generously with poppy seeds. Let rise in warm place (80 to 85°) until doubled, about 45 minutes. Bake in preheated 350° oven 30 to 40 minutes. 2 loaves.

CHRISTMAS CANE COFFEECAKE

1 package active dry yeast
¼ c. warm water
1 c. milk
2 eggs, beaten
4¼ c. sifted flour
½ c. sugar
1 t. salt
1 t. grated lemon rind
1 c. cold butter

Soften yeast in warm water. Scald milk; cool to lukewarm; blend in softened yeast and eggs. Combine flour, sugar, salt and lemon rind. Cut in butter until mixture resembles coarse crumbs. Add yeast mixture; mix well. Dough is soft. Place in greased bowl; cover; refrigerate overnight. Divide dough into thirds. Roll each third on floured surface into a 6 x 15-inch rectangle. Spread ⅓ of Cranberry Filling lengthwise down center of dough in a strip 2 inches wide. Cut dough with scissors from both outer edges toward filling. Make cuts every ½ inch. Do not cut too close to filling. Crisscross pieces of dough over filling. Place on greased cookie sheet. Stretch shaped dough to about 20 inches; curve top to form a cane. Let rise about ½ hour. Bake at 375° about 25 minutes. Frost with thin confectioners' sugar glaze and decorate if desired. Makes 3 canes.

CRANBERRY FILLING

1½ c. finely chopped cranberries
¾ c. sugar
½ c. raisins
⅓ c. chopped pecans
⅓ c. honey
1 t. grated orange rind

Combine all ingredients. Cook over medium heat about 5 minutes. Stir. Cool.

SNACKS

BLUE CHEESE BALL
See color photo opposite

1 8-oz. package cream cheese, softened
4 oz. blue cheese, crumbled
¼ c. chopped green onion
1 t. lemon juice
1 clove garlic, minced
¼ t. pepper
¼ t. salt
½ c. chopped parsley

Combine all ingredients except parsley; blend well. Form mixture into a ball. Roll in chopped parsley. Chill thoroughly.

CHEDDAR CHEESE BALL

1 8-oz. package cream cheese, softened
4 oz. sharp cheddar cheese, grated
1 T. chopped pimiento
¼ t. cayenne pepper
¼ t. salt
1 T. chopped green pepper
1 t. chopped onion
1½ t. Worcestershire sauce
Red Walnuts

Put cream cheese into small mixing bowl; beat until smooth and creamy. Add remaining ingredients except Red Walnuts. Blend well. Shape into a ball, roll in nuts and chill.

RED WALNUTS

½ t. red food coloring
1½ T. warm water
1 c. finely chopped walnuts

Dissolve food coloring in water. Sprinkle over walnuts and stir until all nuts are red. Spread nuts on an ungreased cookie sheet and bake at 250° for 10-15 minutes. Do not allow nuts to brown. If walnuts are not completely dry, turn off oven and allow nuts to remain inside until dry. Cool thoroughly.

SMOKED BEEF DIP

1 t. minced onion
1 T. sherry
1 8-oz. package cream cheese
2 T. mayonnaise
¼ c. stuffed olives, minced
1 3-oz. package smoked beef, minced

Soak onion in sherry until soft. Add remaining ingredients.

Mrs. Roger C. Wilder

CHEESE POPCORN

Vegetable oil
Popcorn
1 t. paprika
1 t. salt or onion or garlic salt
⅓ c. grated cheese

Pour oil to depth of about ⅛ inch in pan. Pour in enough popcorn to cover bottom of pan 1 kernel deep. Cover tightly and place over high heat, shaking until corn stops popping. Combine paprika, salt and grated cheese. Sprinkle over hot corn, mixing so that all kernels are coated.

Edith Pikelny

NIBBLE MIX

1 lb. butter, melted
6 T. Worcestershire sauce
2 t. garlic salt
2 t. onion salt

Place butter in a baking dish and put in roaster or oven to melt. Stir in Worcestershire sauce. Add small boxes of the following.

Rice Chex   **Wheat Chex**
Cheerios   **Pretzel sticks**
1 can mixed nuts

Sprinkle with the garlic and onion salts. Mix. Bake at 225° for 1 hour, stirring occasionally.

Edith Shaska

*Photo opposite
Blue Cheese Ball, this page*

RELISHES, JELLIES AND PRESERVES

HAPPY HOLIDAYS CONSERVE

2 30-oz. cans apricot halves
1 c. glacé mixed fruits
½ c. quartered red glacé cherries
1½ c. sugar
¼ t. salt
¼ t. nutmeg
1 T. grated lemon peel
1 T. grated orange peel
1½ c. finely chopped pecans

Drain apricots, reserving 1½ cups syrup. Coarsely chop the apricots. Place apricots, the 1½ cups apricot syrup and all remaining ingredients except pecans in 6-quart pot. Bring to a boil, stirring occasionally. Reduce heat; simmer uncovered about 25 minutes or until thickened and of desired consistency. Stir in pecans; ladle into hot sterilized jars and seal and lid or cover with paraffin according to manufacturer's directions. Makes about 6 cups.

TILLIE'S WATERMELON PICKLES

7 lbs. watermelon rinds
7 c. sugar
2 c. vinegar
  Cinnamon sticks
  Whole cloves
  Maraschino cherries

Put melon rinds in a large kettle; cover with water. Boil until tender. Combine sugar and vinegar; bring to a boil and pour over rinds. Add cinnamon and cloves to taste. The next morning, drain and bring syrup to a boil again; pour over rinds. On the third morning, drain again. Cut rind into desired shapes. Pack in jars and pour hot syrup over. If desired, add a few maraschino cherries. Seal. *Note:* The cherries will fade if pickles are not used for a long time.

Dorothy Benson

APPLE JELLY

3 lbs. ripe, tart apples
3 c. water
2 T. lemon juice
3 c. sugar

Cut washed, unpeeled, uncored apples into small pieces. Add water, cover and bring to a boil. Simmer for 20 to 25 minutes, until apples are soft. Extract juice; measure. Combine 4 cups apple juice, lemon juice and sugar in a large kettle; stir well. Boil over high heat until mixture reaches 220° and jelly forms a sheet on a metal spoon. Skim off foam; pour jelly immediately into hot sterilized glasses. Seal.

MINT JELLY

1 c. firmly packed mint leaves
1 c. boiling water
3 lbs. ripe, tart apples
3 c. water
2 T. lemon juice
3 c. sugar
  Green food coloring

Pour boiling water over mint leaves and let stand for 1 hour. Press the juice from the leaves. Measure 8 tablespoons of mint extract into a large saucepan. Proceed as for Apple Jelly (above). Before pouring jelly into glasses, tint with food coloring.

BRANDIED APRICOTS
See color photo, page 35

2 30-oz. cans whole apricots
¾ c. brandy
2 cinnamon sticks, broken
6 whole cloves

Drain apricots, reserving 2 cups syrup. In medium saucepan combine syrup with brandy and spices. Bring to a boil, reduce heat and simmer uncovered for 15 minutes. Pour hot syrup over drained apricots in bowl. Cover and chill for 3 to 4 hours or until serving time, or pack into jars immediately.

CHERRY JAM

4 c. pitted sour cherries
¼ c. water
5 c. sugar
1 6-oz. bottle liquid pectin

Combine cherries and water in large kettle. Bring to a boil, then simmer for 15 minutes. Stir in sugar. Bring mixture to a boil; then boil, stirring, for 3 minutes. Stir in pectin. Remove from heat; stir and skim for 5 minutes. Pour into hot sterilized jars. Seal at once.

SWEET ONION RINGS

8 c. sliced onions (about 3 lbs.)
  Boiling water
1 c. distilled white vinegar
1 c. granulated sugar
2 t. salt
½ t. mustard seed

Cook onions in boiling water for 4 minutes; drain. Combine vinegar and remaining ingredients in large saucepan; bring to boil. Add onions; simmer 4 minutes. Continue simmering while quickly packing one clean, hot jar at a time. Fill to within ½ inch of top, making sure vinegar solution covers onions. Cap each jar at once. Process 5 minutes in boiling water bath. Makes 2 to 3 pints.

Sweet Onion Rings, this page

Pack an assortment of jellies in a small wooden crate. Attach a wire handle and, if you wish, stencil a Christmas greeting on the side slats.

Give jellies in decorative heat-proof jars or glasses. Be sure to label with variety, date and your name. If you wish, decorate the jar with colorful stickers or photographs of the kind of fruit used in the jelly.

For a lasting remembrance, give pepper relish with a pepper plant, mint jelly with a mint plant, etc. Long after the cooked gift is gone, the plant will be a reminder of your thoughtfulness. And if you attach the recipe, the recipient will be doubly pleased: she'll be able to make her own relish or jelly from the plant when it matures.

A mouthwatering gift combination is a jar of homemade preserves with a loaf of homemade bread. This is one gift that probably won't last through the holidays, so pack the preserves in an especially pretty jar.

GRAPE BURGUNDY JELLY

See color photo opposite

1½ lbs. fully ripe Concord grapes
¼ c. water
5 c. sugar
1 c. Burgundy wine
½ bottle liquid fruit pectin (3 fl. oz.)

Thoroughly crush the grapes, one layer at a time. Add ¼ cup water; bring to a boil and simmer, covered, for 10 minutes. Place in jelly cloth or bag and squeeze out juice. Measure 2 cups into a large saucepan. Thoroughly mix sugar and wine into juice in saucepan. Place over high heat and bring just to a boil, stirring constantly. Remove from heat. Stir in fruit pectin at once. Skim off foam with metal spoon; pour jelly quickly into glasses. Cover at once with ⅛ inch hot paraffin. Makes about 5½ cups or 7 glasses, 6 fluid ounces each.

CRANBERRY CLARET JELLY

See color photo opposite

3½ c. sugar
1 c. cranberry juice cocktail
1 c. claret wine
½ bottle liquid fruit pectin (3 fl. oz.)

Measure sugar, cranberry juice cocktail and wine into a large saucepan. Stir over medium heat, bringing mixture to just below the boiling point. Continue stirring until the sugar is dissolved, about 5 minutes. Remove from heat. At once stir in fruit pectin and mix well. Skim off foam with metal spoon and pour quickly into glasses. Cover at once with ⅛ inch hot paraffin. Makes about 4 cups or 5 glasses, 6 fluid ounces each.

ORANGE MARMALADE

5 oranges	8½ c. sugar
2 grapefruit	Juice of
12 c. cold water	2 lemons

Slice fruit thin and cut in small pieces. Add water and boil for 1 hour or until fruit is soft. Add sugar and boil for 45 minutes. Add lemon juice. Boil until thick and 2 drops fall from spoon when tested. Pour into glasses and seal with paraffin.

Bina Sterling

APRICOT MUSCATEL JELLY

See color photo opposite

3½ c. sugar
1 c. muscatel wine
1 c. apricot nectar
2 T. lemon juice
½ bottle liquid fruit pectin (3 fl. oz.)

Measure sugar, wine, nectar and juice into large saucepan. Stir over medium heat, bringing mixture to just below the boiling point. Continue stirring until the sugar is dissolved, about 5 minutes. Remove from heat. At once stir in fruit pectin and mix well. Skim off foam with metal spoon and pour quickly into glasses. Cover at once with ⅛ inch hot paraffin. Makes about 4 cups or 5 glasses, 6 fluid ounces each.

BAKED APPLE BUTTER

10 lbs. apples	1 T. cinnamon
1½ qts. cider	1 T. nutmeg
1 T. cloves	5 lbs. sugar

Peel, core and quarter apples, adding enough water to cover. Simmer in a large pot until they reach sauce consistency. Stir in the cider, cloves, cinnamon, nutmeg and sugar. Pour the mixture into an enameled roasting pan. Cover. Place in a 350° oven. Stir occasionally, until the mixture boils. Then turn down the oven to 250° and bake 5 hours, or overnight. Ladle the thick apple butter into sterilized jars and seal for storage.

Rosalie L. Kennedy

RED PEPPER RELISH

1 peck red peppers
3 lbs. white sugar
3 pts. white vinegar
2 oz. mustard seeds

Remove seeds from peppers and grind peppers with a fine cutter. Wash mustard seeds and soak in hot water about 2 to 3 hours. Place all ingredients together and cook slowly until mixture jellies from a spoon. Watch carefully and stir often so it does not scorch. Use low heat.

Eleanore B. Malec

Photo opposite
Apricot Muscatel Jelly, this page
Cranberry Claret Jelly, this page
Grape Burgundy Jelly, this page
Lemon Fruit-Jell Candy, page 11
Cranberry Jelly Candy, page 11

From our house
to your house
for this
holiday season
B.

BEVERAGES

HOT CRANBERRY PUNCH

4 c. water
½ lb. cranberries
2 c. sugar
1 large orange
1½ inches stick cinnamon
1 t. whole cloves
1 qt. apple juice
1 pt. apple wine

Combine water, cranberries and sugar in a saucepan. Cut orange into quarters and add. Combine spices in a cheesecloth bag; add. Bring mixture to a boil and simmer for 5 minutes, constantly crushing berries with a spoon. Remove spices and orange sections. Strain cranberry mixture. Set berries aside for use as a relish. Combine liquid and apple juice; heat to boiling. Add apple wine and heat but do not boil. Serve immediately in a heated bowl. *Note:* When making this punch as a gift, prepare as above except do not add wine. Give punch and wine in separate bottles; include directions for heating and serving.

SPARKLING PUNCH

½ c. sugar
1 c. water
4 cinnamon sticks
6 whole cloves
1 c. lemon juice, chilled
½ c. lime juice, chilled
2 c. orange juice, chilled
1 46-oz. can apricot nectar, chilled
6 7-oz. bottles 7-Up, chilled
1 lemon
1 lime

Combine sugar, water, cinnamon and cloves in saucepan, simmer for 5 minutes. Set aside for several hours or longer. Strain syrup; discard spices. At serving time, combine syrup and chilled juices in a large punch bowl. Slowly pour in 7-Up. Add ice if desired. Garnish with slices of lemon and lime.

MINT PUNCH

½ c. fresh mint
1 qt. water
4 c. sugar
¼ t. salt
¼ t. green food coloring
1 qt. lemon juice
4 16-oz. bottles ginger ale

Reserve a few sprigs of mint for garnish. Combine remaining mint with 1 cup water in blender. Blend for 30 seconds. Combine mint mixture with sugar and remaining water; simmer for 5 minutes. Strain; add salt, food coloring and lemon juice. Chill thoroughly. To serve, mix mint mixture gently with chilled ginger ale. Garnish with reserved mint.

CHRISTMAS PUNCH

2 c. boiling water
¾ c. sugar
½ t. cinnamon
¼ t. nutmeg
¼ t. salt
2 16-oz. bottles cranberry juice cocktail
1 6-oz. can frozen pineapple concentrate
1 c. cold water
2 12-oz. bottles carbonated water

Pour boiling water over sugar, cinnamon, nutmeg and salt; stir to dissolve. Chill thoroughly. To serve, combine with remaining ingredients in punch bowl. Add ice if desired.

PINK FRUIT PUNCH

6 c. sugar
6 c. water
2 packages strawberry Kool-Aid
1 12-oz. can frozen lemon juice
1 12-oz. can frozen orange juice
1 46-oz. can pineapple juice

Combine sugar and water. Boil for 5 minutes. Cool. Add remaining ingredients. When ready to serve the punch add 2 quarts of ginger ale plus enough water to make three gallons.

Mrs. Robert E. O'Leary

BLOSSOM BOUQUET

1 qt. elderberry blossoms
1 gallon boiling water
3 lbs. sugar
½ c. yeast
1 lb. raisins
1 orange
1 lemon

Soak blossoms in boiling water for 1½ hours. Then strain and boil for 10 minutes with sugar. Cool to lukewarm. Add yeast, raisins and cut up orange and lemon. Pour into a 5-gallon crock and allow to ferment for at least 24 hours. Mixture may take up to 6 days to clarify. When fermenting stage is done, wine can be bottled, but do not cap immediately. Place in a cool basement. The longer the wine is stored, the more delicious and clear it becomes.

Marie De Amhoggi

GRAPE WINE

3 6-oz. cans frozen grape juice
5 c. sugar
1 t. dry yeast

Combine ingredients; mix until dissolved. Pour into a gallon jug; fill with water to near top. Tie a balloon tightly onto the top of jug. Let mixture stand 21 days, then bottle.

Gertrude Hogate

GRAPEFRUIT WINE

2 qts. grapefruit juice
1 lb. sugar

Combine juice and sugar. Pour mixture into jug; cover with 2 layers or cheesecloth. Place jug in a small pan to catch overflow. Let stand at room temperature for 4 weeks or until fermenting has stopped. Strain wine through cheesecloth, avoiding the sediment. Strain again through filter paper. Pour into bottles; cork.

Homemade wine is a Christmas gift that's sure to be appreciated. But it needs sufficient time to ferment, so don't try to make wine as a last-minute Christmas gift.

An attractive and lasting gift to complement a bottle of homemade wine is an ice bucket.

Wines or punches can be decorated with pieces of the same fruit used in making them. If it's a small fruit, like grapes or cranberries, attach a few pieces to the ribbon you use to tie the gift. If it's a large fruit, you may prefer to decorate the label with colorful photographs of the fruit instead.

A decanter is a lovely, lasting gift to go with a bottle of homemade wine. If you're giving punch to a special friend, give a punchbowl too.

Punches that do not include carbonated beverages can be prepared in advance and given in a decorative bottle. For punches with carbonated ingredients, prepare the rest of the punch, bottle it and give it along with unopened bottles of carbonated beverages. Be sure to include directions for mixing and serving.

DECORATING WITH FOOD

FESTIVE APRICOT ORNAMENT

See color photo opposite

1 Styrofoam ball, about 4 inches in diameter
  Round toothpicks
  White glue
7 inches orange cord for hanging-loop
  Straight pins
  Dark raisins
1 10½-oz. package miniature marshmallows
1 8-oz. package California dried apricot halves
½ yard ribbon, ½ inch in diameter (green or orange)

Make tiny hole in top of ball with toothpick; fill with glue. Tie cord to make 3½-inch loop; push straight pin through knot and into hole in top of ball with toothpick half. Leave toothpick in ball to secure loop; let dry thoroughly. Attach a row of dark raisins around center of ball with straight pins. You will need about 2 dozen raisins. On both sides of raisin row, make a row of miniature marshmallows; attach with straight pins. Reserve 2 apricot halves. Cut the remaining halves into two pieces each. Working from marshmallow row, arrange apricot semi-circles in circular fashion, with straight cut side against marshmallows. Be sure to place apricot pieces end to end. Repeat with two more rows. Make an apricot flower in center by arranging three apricot pieces in a circle, ends touching, forming a triangular space in center. Secure each petal with a straight pin. Make center of flower by placing one dried apricot half on top of petals; place raisin in center of apricot and attach both with straight pin. Decorate other side of ball in same way. Tie ribbon into 4-inch bow; attach with pins near hanging loop. Makes a festive tree hanging!

AN OLD-FASHIONED BELL

See color photo opposite

1 Styrofoam bell, about 3 inches in diameter
  Round toothpicks
  White glue
  Orange tassel, about 3 inches long
  Straight pins
7 inches orange cord for hanging loop
  Orange beads, about ¼ inch long
  Orange spray paint (optional)
  Round orange sequins, about ⅝ inch in diameter
1 8-oz. package California dried apricot halves

Make tiny hole in the center of both top and bottom of bell with toothpick; fill with glue. Fasten tassel by pushing straight pin through tassel, then into bottom of bell with toothpick half; leave pick in bell to secure tassel. Attach hanging loop by tying cord to make 3½-inch loop; push straight pin through knot and into hole in top of bell with toothpick half. Leave toothpick in bell to secure loop. Let dry thoroughly. Spray bell with orange paint, if desired; hang on nail until completely dry. (Paint avoids white Styrofoam showing through.) Decorate the top of bell with two circular rows of sequins as follows: Thread straight pin through one orange bead, then through sequin; attach in circular pattern, covering top 2-inch area of bell around cord loop. Cover remaining surface of bell with dried apricot halves arranged in circular pattern; secure apricot halves in place with pins, inserted at top of each apricot half. Hang in window or on the Christmas tree. Or, turn it into a "Kissin' Bell": Using straight pins, fasten a spring of mistletoe near tassel of bell. Hang with thumbtack in doorway.

When mailing decorations made of food, use a sturdy cardboard box and plenty of filler. Be sure to mark the package FRAGILE.

Trim-A-Tree Cookies don't have to be restricted to use on the tree itself. To give your home a festive holiday look, try hanging them from a stairway banister along with sprigs of artificial holly.

For a last-minute gift with a personal touch, tie pieces of candy to an inexpensive artificial wreath. Children will love it!

Decorations made of perishable food can be used for only one season—be sure to explain this when giving them to friends. You can preserve some decorations by shellacking them.

If you give Trim-A-Tree Cookies, include an airtight container for storing them between holiday seasons. Otherwise they will become soft or soggy.

POPCORN TREE

½ c. water
½ c. light corn syrup
1 c. sugar
8 c. popped corn
1 Styrofoam cone, 12 inches high
   Wooden toothpicks
   Gumdrops

Combine water, corn syrup and sugar in saucepan. Cook without stirring over medium heat until syrup reaches soft ball stage (240°). Pour syrup over popcorn, mixing with hands until popcorn is coated. Quickly form small amounts of mixture into balls of various sizes. To assemble tree, place a toothpick in each ball and stick into cone to form tree. Use smaller balls for the top of the tree. Insert gumdrops for ornaments.

SPICE BALL

1 Styrofoam ball, 3-4 inches in diameter
   White glue
   Whole cloves
   Whole anise seeds
   Whole poppy seeds
   Whole celery seeds
   Whole caraway seeds
   Ground cinnamon
   Ground paprika
   Ground mustard
   Curry powder
1 sprig plastic holly or pine
7½ inches red velvet ribbon

With a pencil or crayon, mark Styrofoam ball into 8 equal sections. Along these lines, insert whole cloves to outline the sections. Cover one section at a time with white glue, then sprinkle with one of the spices until Styrofoam is completely covered. Alternate sections of whole and ground spices. Let the ball dry, then decorate with a sprig of holly or pine. Make a loop of the ribbon and pin it to the ball so it can be hung. *Note:* Different spices can be substituted for those listed. Experiment until you find a combination with the fragrance and appearance you like best.

GINGHAM WREATH

1 Styrofoam wreath, about 4 inches
   in diameter
   Round toothpicks
   White glue
7 inches orange cord, for hanging-loop
   Straight pins
1 8-oz. package California dried apricot
   halves
   Gold foil decorator leaves
1 yard 1½-inch gingham ribbon (green or
   gold check)
   Staples for bow

Make tiny hole in top of wreath with toothpick; fill with glue. Tie cord to make 3½-inch loop; push straight pin through knot and into hole in top of wreath with toothpick half. Leave toothpick in wreath to secure loop; let dry thoroughly. Cut 12 apricot halves into 2 pieces each. Attach 2 semicircle pieces with straight pins, directly across from each other on outside edge of wreath, giving scalloped edge to wreath. Some Styrofoam area will show between the 2 apricot pieces. Place apricot half on top of these 2 pieces, covering this white area and forming a cluster of apricots. Repeat to make 11 or 12 more clusters, attached end to end. Entire outside surface of wreath will be covered. Attach gold foil leaves between each cluster of apricots. To make bow, cut 3 pieces of ribbon one 8 inches, one 10 inches and one 15 inches long. Using 8-inch piece, make a loop 3½ inches in length, allowing ends of ribbon to meet in center of loop overlapping about 1 inch. Secure with staple. Repeat with 10-inch piece, making a loop about 4½ inches long. To form bow, place 3½-inch loop on top of 4½-inch loop. Pinch loops together in center, then tie with the 15-inch piece of ribbon around loops. Secure bow to bottom of wreath with straight pins.

TRIM-A-TREE COOKIES

See color photo, page 62

4 c. unsifted flour
1 c. salt
1½ c. water
   Wire for hooks
   Water colors, Tempera or Acrylic
   paints
   Clear fixative

Combine flour, salt and water in a large mixing bowl. Mix thoroughly with hands. Add more water if dough is too stiff. Shape into a ball. Knead dough about 5 minutes or until smooth. Keep covered with foil or plastic wrap as dough dries out quickly. Roll dough about ¼ inch thick on lightly floured surface. Cut into desired shapes with sharp knife or cookie cutter. Place on ungreased cookie sheets. Insert wire into cookie. A paper clip or hair pin will also work. This will serve as a hook for hanging on tree. Bake in oven 350° until thoroughly dried and hard, about 1 hour depending on thickness. Cool. Paint as desired. Allow to dry. Spray completely with fixative. *Note:* This recipe must not be doubled or halved. Cookies often puff up during baking. **These cookies are not edible.**

WAGON BREAD LOAF

1 loaf frozen bread dough
4 cooked doughnuts
   High gloss varnish
   White glue
   Wooden picks
   Long pretzel
   Small plastic flowers

Follow instructions for thawing bread. Bake in 150° oven 6 hours. Bake the cooked doughnuts in 150° oven 3 hours. Let both set out 3 days to dry. Brush with 1 coat of varnish, letting dry 24 hours; repeat varnish step two more times. For wheels, bore a hole with a skewer into doughnuts and sides of bread. Place wooden picks in bored hole; attach and glue. Make another hole in center front of bread for handle and attach pretzel with glue. Glue flowers into holes of doughnut. Pour glue down top center of bread and lay 10 or 12 flowers (stems cut off) on top of the glue.

Trim-A-Tree Cookies, page 61

Yuletime brings to you and me
The season for a cookie tree
Bedecked with goodies to bring surprise
And a wishful shine to childrens' eyes.

On a low table our cookie tree stands
Within the reach of eager hands,
A glimmering, shimmering treasury
Of Christmas hospitality.

Mary A. Selden

62

INDEX